ᴖ Bloomfield Avenue

Cowley Publications is a ministry of the brothers of the Society of Saint John the Evangelist, a monastic order in the Episcopal Church. Our mission is to provide books and resources for those seeking spiritual and theological formation. Cowley Publications is committed to developing a new generation of writers and teachers who will encourage people to think and pray in new ways about spirituality, reconciliation, and the future.

Mercadante family shop on Bloomfield Avenue, Newark, New Jersey.
Photo by Linda Mercadante.

Bloomfield Avenue

A Jewish-Catholic Jersey Girl's Spiritual Journey

Linda Mercadante

Cowley Publications

CAMBRIDGE, MASSACHUSETTS

Published in the United States of America by Cowley Publications, a division of the Society of Saint John the Evangelist. No portion of this book may be reproduced, stored in or introduced into a retrieval system, or transmitted, in any form or by any means—including photocopying—without the prior written permission of Cowley Publications, except in the case of brief quotations embedded in critical articles and reviews.

Library of Congress Cataloging-in-Publication Data

Mercadante, Linda A.
  Bloomfield Avenue : a Jewish-Catholic Jersey girl's spiritual journey / Linda Mercadante.
    p. cm.
  Includes bibliographical references.
  ISBN-10: 1-56101-278-5 ISBN-13: 978-1-56101-278-7 (pbk. : alk. paper)
  1. Mercadante, Linda A., 1947– 2. Children of interfaith marriage—United States—Biography. 3. Protestant converts—United States—Biography. 4. Presbyterian Church (U.S.A.)—Clergy—Biography. I. Title.
  BX9225.M44A3   2006
  248.2'44092—dc22
[B]
                                                        2006015629

Scripture quotations are taken from The New Revised Standard Version of the Bible, © 1989, by the Division of Christian Education of the National Council of the Churches of Christ in the United States of America. Used by permission.

Cover photo: Linda Mercadante
Cover design: Rini Twait of Graphical Jazz, L.L.C.
Interior design: Wendy Holdman

This book was printed in the United States of America on acid-free paper.

Cowley Publications
4 Brattle Street
Cambridge, Massachusetts 02138
800-225-1534 • www.cowley.org

DEDICATION

To David and Joe, who have helped me keep (both) feet on the ground.

Contents

Acknowledgments

After my father's funeral, I had writer's block. One mentor, Patrick Henry, said "When you are blocked, write about the block." Out of that advice came a short article on how healing had happened for me during the funeral. My article appeared in *The Christian Century* and was even reprinted in a Texas newspaper. So many people said the article helped them think about their own mixed backgrounds, that I knew I would eventually have to write a book. When the Workgroup on Constructive Theology insisted I write an article on Newark, New Jersey, I did the research and gained new respect for my background. Out of these two sources, the present book emerged.

But between beginning and ending this manuscript, I fell down some stairs, broke my heel, later my elbow, and ended up having nine surgeries and a three-year recovery period. Sometimes—with foot or arm propped up—working on this manuscript was the only thing that kept making sense to me. More important, during that period, I got to know the kindness of Joseph Mas, a Cuban refugee and—by the time you read this—my husband. His empathy, as well as his understanding of immigrant roots and assimilation, helped me stay on task and complete the work.

Also crucial has been a key character in this narrative, Dorianne Perrucci, who provided essential encouragement, insisting the project had value even when my three guilt-flavors made me doubt it. I have many others to thank as well. Especially, I appreciate my friends, colleagues and students who read parts of the manuscript and made very helpful comments. Among them are: Dori Perrucci, Joseph Mas, Patrick Henry, Robert Rakestraw, Susan Ritchie, Rosemarie Rossetti, Pamela Moore, and Rhoda Isaac. I also thank First Presbyterian Church of Delaware (Ohio), St. John's Episcopal Church (Worthington, Ohio), First Unitarian Universalist Church (Columbus, Ohio), and Kirkridge Retreat Center, for inviting me to give readings from the manuscript. I also thank the participants in my various memoir-writing workshops who—by writing their stories—deepened my understanding that we all must find the meaning of our own lives.

Special thanks are due Tatha Wiley. Her support and persistent championing of the project were key, especially since she linked me up with Michael Wilt at Cowley Publications. Michael has been wonderful to work with, and I especially thank him for assigning Johnny Ross to be my editor. Johnny's insightful comments helped me to further clarify and unify the narrative.

I have to thank my son, David, for resolutely refusing to get involved in this book, even though he is mentioned in it. As a true teenager and son, he kept me from having delusions of grandeur while, at the same time, easily accepting all the time I spent at the computer. I would also like to thank my seminary, The Methodist Theological School in Ohio, for giving me the intellectual and emotional freedom over the last nineteen years to write about whatever I find compelling and relevant.

I am likely leaving out many friends and family who listened to me talk about the project, read snippets, and kept inquiring about the progress of the manuscript. Thanks to them and to all the people mentioned in this book. Although

I have tried resolutely to present things exactly as I remember them—not embellishing or making up anything—please remember that memory is selective and a memoir is a personal narrative. Beyond that, I offer the story to anyone with a complicated or mixed background—whether religious, ethnic, racial, national, or other—to suggest that the Spirit can make you a new creation and whole.

5 Bloomfield Avenue

Chapter One

The Little Italian Girl
Who Wanted a Crucifix

When I was a child, all I really wanted was a crucifix on a chain. Of course, if someone had offered me a St. Christopher medal, some rosary beads, or maybe a nice prayer book, I would have taken it gladly. But I was most desperate for a tiny crucifix to hang around my neck. What made it so hard was that no one knew. And I couldn't tell.

In my childhood neighborhood—the North Ward of Newark, New Jersey, during the 1950s and 60s—Catholicism, food, and Italian culture were all mixed together. In fact, if you were willing to ignore the diesel smells, planes on approach to Newark airport, and traffic heading downtown, you'd almost think you were in Italy.

I lived on a busy street, Bloomfield Avenue, which went right through the heart of the Italian neighborhood on its way out of town toward the suburbs. Lined with small family businesses, this street gave off enough smells, sights, and sounds to put you in a good mood. Spicy fragrances wafted through the door of Mama Lucia's restaurant, fresh-baked bread called to you from Calandra's, and few could pass Celentano's display of plump, homemade raviolis without thinking ahead to Sunday dinner. With this and the air of *scungilli*, pizza, espresso, and pastry everywhere, it was hard to walk down the street without getting hungry.

It wasn't a quiet neighborhood, either. The sidewalk was crowded with shoppers, kids playing ball, and people just hanging around outside the taverns, pizza parlors, bakeries, shoe repair shops, and restaurants. Old men sat on beat-up wooden chairs outside their social clubs, playing cards, cutting deals, and commenting on passers-by. Grandmothers dressed in black stood alongside the produce truck that wended its way through the neighborhood, haggling with the man about the price of his tomatoes. Anywhere you went, if two people got to arguing, they'd soon be making the sign of the cross and appealing to the Madonna for support.

My family's business, Ditta Ferrara French and Italian Pastry Shop, was right in the middle of everything. To the fragrant mix on Bloomfield Avenue, our business contributed rum, dough, almond oil, homemade lemon ice, and frying *zeppole*. We added sounds, too: in the back of the shop, Italian opera played on the radio, and in front, determined customers called out their orders in Italian.

My father, Gene, and his twin brother, Roger, had bought the pastry shop from another Italian family after they were discharged from the U.S. Army at the end of World War II. Since our property also included three small apartments, the two twin brothers lived right there with their wives, children, and their mother, my Grandma Angela.

The shop was as much my home as our apartment upstairs. I felt proud every time I looked at our large, red and black sign that stuck out over the sidewalk, with *"Mercadante Brothers"* in white neon lights just below the store name. From an early age I was put to work, selling pastries as soon as I could reach the counter and often sent to do errands at the other shops. It always amazed me how the other shopkeepers on Bloomfield Avenue knew who I was. I wasn't very talkative and often didn't identify myself, but somehow they recognized me as part of the bakery. Maybe it was because, like everyone else in our business, I was always covered in a layer of flour, studded with blobs of custard cream, and smelled just like the bakery.

"You're from Ferrara's," said Rocco, the owner of the Italian pork store at the end of our block, when I walked in. He knew what I needed, without my having to say anything. My family loved sausage and peppers.

"Did they tell you to get two pounds?" he asked. "What about bread?" I was a little shy and simply nodded yes to both questions, showing him the cash I held tightly in my small hand.

"Okay, here, this is the kind your mother likes, sweet, not hot," Rocco would say as he wrapped up the shiny, fat, reddish links in waxed paper and put them in the bag next to the long loaf. Often, by the time I got back to our pastry shop, the heel of the crusty bread—which always seemed to stick out of the bag right at mouth level—was gone.

"Gerry," my father would say to my mother, chuckling as he took the bag from me, "I think a little mouse got into our bread." My father liked someone with a healthy appetite.

My father's generous attitude toward food extended to everyone who worked in our store. We always had many members of our extended family working there as well as various backroom helpers and salesgirls. All day long there was food around for everyone. Each evening, our workers almost always left with several boxes of baked goods under their arms.

"Daddy," I once asked my father, "won't the workers eat up all the pastries and we won't have anything to sell?"

"Oh, don't worry about that, Linda," my father said, smiling. "They get tired of it after awhile."

Maybe that's why I, along with my brother Eugene and Uncle Roger's daughters, Angela and Susan, had an entirely different attitude toward Italian pastry than our customers or workers. The four of us made it a point of honor never to eat our parents' products. We were like medieval ascetics when it came to dessert, for no matter how many rum *babas, sfogliatelle, cannoli* or rum cakes they piled in front of us, we turned up our noses, shook our heads, and said a determined "Yuk!"

Instead, I ate other kinds of pastry rebelliously. On my way home after school and before I re-entered our Italian neighborhood, I would stop at a little American grocery and buy a Ring-Ding. I tried to eat it before I got to our store, but sometimes my father would find the wrapper in my pocket or an obvious remnant on my dress. At these times and others when I rejected his creations, he didn't act hurt. But the next time he caught me eating something "American," like a brownie, he would say, "You know, Linda, they make those things with the sweepings off the floor."

Maybe this was my first recognition that there was a world beyond our little Italian island. Still, I felt secure in my environment, and even better, I was almost never lonely. It took a lot of people to run the bakery and it was open from early morning to late at night 364 days a year. There was always someone to talk to and at mealtimes often an aunt, an uncle, or a cousin would join us at the table. And always my grandmother was there.

Grandma Angela had two other children besides Gene and Roger, an older sister, Mary, and a younger brother, Pat. Both of them were also involved in the bakery business. All sixteen of us, nine adults and seven children, lived in and around Newark and visited back and forth constantly. At holidays, for each cousin's birthday, and for any other event that could be celebrated, the whole extended family got together.

Our tiny apartment, a modest kitchen, living/dining

room, three little bedrooms and one bath, would regularly hold twenty-five or more people, because oftentimes other families or friends—perhaps someone's in-laws—would be included, too. I loved those parties more than anything, cousins running and squealing, adults talking and laughing, and lots of food. The apartments, the family, and our bakery were a whole world for me. I had almost everything I needed.

Crosses

Surrounding my little world was a sea of Catholicism. The North Ward, from the late 1800s until the riots of 1967, had one of the largest Italian-heritage populations on the East Coast. Being Catholic was just part of being Italian. Most everyone—men, women, and children—had a cross or medal on a gold chain around his or her neck. Some also had a little horn, a charm against the evil eye. Nevertheless, no matter how superstitious they were or how often—or seldom—they went to mass, everyone was confidently Catholic.

Most stores on our street had a large picture of Jesus with his heart exposed, vivid red and bleeding for your sins, prominently displayed right behind the counter where everyone could see it. Our bakery was a bit different and had, instead, a collection of holy cards that my grandmother would periodically stick up behind cake signs, the telephone, or anywhere else she had a fancy to bless, protect, or decorate.

Grandma Angela's apartment, like the homes of my friends, displayed religious statues, burning holy candles, and other religious icons just about everywhere. Our neighborhood also specialized in Virgin Mary grottos. Behind our commercial street were several blocks of modest, frame row houses. Residents who could not afford a commercial grotto for their front yard would often take a discarded bathtub, cut it in half, paint it sky-blue, and stand it on end to shelter the Virgin, usually dressed in matching blue, with downcast eyes and a holy look on her face.

All this made an impression on me, but nothing so much as Sacred Heart Cathedral. This immense church—the largest French Gothic structure in North America—was only a few blocks away from our store. It stood at the head of huge Branch Brook Park and was visible from many points in the neighborhood. North Warders took particular pride in this cathedral, for it was built over many years by the hands and pennies of immigrants. I loved to see Sacred Heart towering above all the other buildings, silhouetted so high against the sky you almost got a stiff neck looking up at it.

My mother and I used to walk by the cathedral every time she took me to play in the park. She always seemed to be in a hurry as we passed and somewhat annoyed. When I tried to linger, asking questions, looking at the carvings, she would pull me along with a brisk jerk. I couldn't understand how she could ignore such an imposing and inspiring structure, but I stared at it in awe each time.

Its twin steeples seemed so free up there in the sky, way above the city dirt and noise. They seemed to promise to lift me up to a clean, serene place. I wanted to climb those cathedral towers; I wanted to go to the top and look out over the world and make some sense of it. But my mother would always hustle me along.

"Come on. Daddy doesn't want me to be gone too long," she'd say, thinking about the work she had left behind in the bakery in order to take me to the park.

But religion always followed us back to the bakery, because our store offered a regular liturgical year in food. We were like the church of pastry, marking each important saint's day and other special events of the Catholic year with a specific baked item. Besides the *cannoli, sfogliatelle, babas,* rum cakes, *pignoli* cookies, and other staples that were available all year, my father and uncle made *struffoli* at Christmas, *zeppole* on St. Joseph's Day (March 19), *pastiera* at Easter, and many other specialties depending upon the season.

In addition, cakes and pastries were always needed for the many first communions, confirmations, ordinations, and feast days celebrated in the Ward. On Sundays, our store was often the first stop after mass. We were so busy that customers would take a number and wait in a long line that sometimes stretched out the door. I liked the bustle in our store but vaguely resented the fact that everyone else got to relax and celebrate on Sunday, while it was the busiest day of the week for us.

Because of the business, my Italian relatives often missed mass on Sunday, especially during the busy holiday seasons. Nevertheless, they seemed quite secure in their Catholicism and regarded missing church as an unavoidable occupational hazard. In their practicality about religion, they resembled the other Italian Catholics in my neighborhood, who had a more relaxed attitude to the rules of religion than the more piously legalistic German and Irish Catholics in the Ward. But relaxed or not, they proudly displayed their Catholicism. All my aunts, uncles and cousins owned a full complement of crosses, medals, rosary beads, holy cards, and prayer books. Their homes displayed crucifixes and religious pictures, holy candles, and small saint statues.

Check Your Religion at the Door

The contrast between my relatives' conspicuously Catholic homes and my parents' apartment was stark. To me, our home felt barren, for it was devoid of anything that even suggested spirituality. From early on, I could tell we were different. My parents had what was referred to—always in hushed tones, when it was mentioned at all—as a "mixed marriage." My mother, Gertrude, known as Gerry, was Jewish, from Brooklyn, of second-generation Russian-Austrian immigrant roots.

My parents had met at a concert in Manhattan. It was the 1940s, and my father, an Army master sergeant, was in uniform. Because of the social dislocation of war, ethnic groups that did not usually mix began to meet. I don't know what made them date outside their own cultures, but they quickly fell in love. Gerry was attracted to this kind, soft-spoken, handsome Italian immigrant, and Gene was drawn to this intelligent, urbane Jewish woman.

I think something else drew them—a common experience that transcended their different cultures. Both had been raised by their mothers, without the presence of their fathers or much money. My mother's father had deserted the family during the Depression. Morris, a Russian immigrant, had courted Gussie, my Jewish grandmother, very ardently. She was pretty and had many suitors but was impressed by Morris's perseverance. If he was that attentive, she figured, he would make a good husband. Gussie did not listen when Morris's own sister warned that her insistent suitor was the "black sheep" of the family—and a womanizer. A determined young woman, Gussie was sure she could reform him. She couldn't—and from the beginning their married life was stormy.

Although they had two girls, Morris continued to chase other women. Finally, after years of this, one day he just went off with one of them, moving to upstate New York and then to Florida. They never divorced, he rarely sent any money, and she never got over it. Forever after, whenever his name was mentioned in our family—which was very infrequently— someone invariably would say, with feeling, "That rat."

My father had a similar story in his background. His

parents, Dominic and Angela, had come to America in the early 1900s, part of the huge wave of European immigrants. She had married him impetuously when he promised to take her to America—even though he was younger and, according to her family, of a lesser class than they. They landed in New York, and Dominic liked America right away. He worked hard and was soon successful as a realtor, a travel agent, a private detective, and any other respectable work he could get.

But Angela was a woman with very strong opinions and emotions. She hated America almost as quickly as her husband loved it. After a few years, she insisted on returning to Italy with their oldest child, Marietta, and the twin sons she had just given birth to in America. She explained to Dominic that she had to help her family back home, but once she got back to their village, she became immoveable. Therefore, although my father, Egidio, and his twin, Ruggiero, were born in the U.S., they spent their entire childhood in Italy.

Dominic went back to Italy at least once during the next couple of years, trying to persuade Angela to do her wifely duty and come back with him. He stayed long enough to conceive another son, Pasquale. But it finally became obvious that stubborn Angela was not going to budge. So all four of their children grew up in San Vitaliano, a small village outside of Naples, without their father, living poorly but sustained by Angela's family.

When the twins became sixteen, Angela decided to send them to America to check up on her husband. She had heard that Dominic had started a new family in America. The boys found him living on his own in New Jersey, but the root of bitterness inspired by Angela prevented them from establishing much of a relationship. The twins were supposed to return to their mother in Italy, but, like their father before them, they loved it here and decided to stay. They were afraid to tell their formidable mother of their decision, however, so one day Angela received a letter from her sister-in-law, who lived in Meriden, Connecticut.

"If you don't want to lose your sons, too," she wrote, "you had better get over here."

Angela might be able to survive without a husband, but she could not live without her twin sons. She didn't want to live in America, but her boys were clearly not going to return to Italy. So finally, at age forty-eight, Angela allowed them to send for her, their older sister, and little brother. But Angela's timing was way off. The exclusive immigration law of 1924 had just been passed, establishing very low quotas for immigrants from southern and eastern Europe. Those who came before the law was passed, hoping to earn money to bring the rest of the family over in time, often ended up being split apart from their relatives for decades or permanently.

But Angela was lucky and was able to secure a short-term visitor's permit to visit her husband and sons. When it expired a year later, she did not leave. If she had wanted to stay permanently and legally, she would have had to exit the country and wait many years on the chance to secure a slot in the quota. But family was too important for her to take this chance. So she remained in a legal limbo for the rest of her life. She could not become naturalized, call attention to herself, or take a chance on leaving the country. She never saw her parents, relatives, or native land again.

Her husband, Dominic, wanted the whole family together, so he made another attempt to reconcile with Angela. One day, girding up his courage, he came to see her with flowers in his arms. But his wife, known for her rages, pushed him down the stairs, sending the flowers and her husband flying. She was proud of that story, one aunt told me, because she thought it showed that she was desirable. But they never got together again.

With similar histories, my parents were determined that their marriage would last. In fact, they believed that family, for all its imperfections, was the only thing you could trust in this world. Indeed, for all the differences between Jews and Italians, marriages between the two groups often work because of the shared values of family loyalty, warmth, and love of home. For their whole married lives my parents spent almost twenty-four hours a day together working hard to make their relationship different from those of their respective parents. Part of their strong belief in family, however, also came out of the discrimination both had experienced because of their religious and ethnic groups.

"When I was just off the boat," my father would say, "Irish boys waited for us around every corner, and they would chase us home, trying to beat us up."

My mother would add, "And even though I grew up in New York, there was still prejudice. In fact, when my mother married my father, because he was from Russia and not a citizen, she lost her citizenship and had to qualify all over again."

All these similarities between Gene and Gerry didn't count for anything with their respective families, though. There had never been a "mixed marriage" in either family and the prospect was repellent. In their circles, such a defiant act usually led to isolation for the couple. Angela had a brother in Italy who was a priest, and she was the most devout member of the family. So she was vociferously against the union and did all she could to discourage it, even cursing my mother to death, right to her face at their first meeting. I guess she figured that if someone was going to hell anyway, it didn't matter what you said to them.

Although my father frequently mentioned that Italians and Jews got along well in Italy—and later he could proudly relate how during World War II Italians took many risks to save Jews—somehow Grandma Angela did not model that attitude. In fact, she had little regard for anyone who wasn't from her part of Italy. This kind of provincialism, while not unknown then, was a holdover from when Italians did not identify themselves as such but as *Napolitano, Siciliano, Abruzzese,* and looked at those from other areas with suspicion. In fact, it was the experience of American prejudice against these immigrants that threw Italians from many different areas into common neighborhoods and began a larger ethnic identification. But my Italian grandmother, who had lived her entire pre-immigration life in one southern Italian village, was from the old school.

My Jewish grandmother, Augusta—"Gussie"—was the child of Jewish-Austrian immigrants. Although not orthodox, Gussie embraced her heritage. After Morris left, Gussie raised her two girls in the Jewish section of Brooklyn, helped by family and friends. I always marveled that they had survived at all, since Gussie was already going blind and deaf when her husband left. When I see today how hard it is for single mothers to manage, I can't imagine how they could have made it in the days before Medicaid, welfare, and other social supports. No wonder my mother regarded Franklin Delano Roosevelt—the president who instituted many social reforms and helped the country through the Depression— as almost a messiah.

Once the two girls became adults, Gussie lived in her own apartment, even though either daughter would have taken her in. She "didn't want to be a burden," she said. Besides, everyone could see that she was a survivor and proud of her independence. However, there was one thing Gussie wasn't prepared for. Having lived among Jews all her life, Gussie entered uncharted territory when her oldest daughter brought home a Gentile. As she got to know him, Gussie could tell that this gentle Italian man might be a good choice for Gerry. Still, Gussie was hesitant. For even though she liked

Gene, she was concerned about this non-traditional pairing. "What would the children be?" she wondered.

Over both their mothers' opposition, my parents married anyway. They had a small civil ceremony with none of the usual ethnic celebration. There was no *huppa* or breaking of the glass for the Jewish side, no mass or blessing by a priest for the Catholics. Out of both families, only my mother's sister, Roslyn, attended the wedding. Since it was wartime, my father returned to duty right away and my mother followed, moving with him to Buffalo and then Louisiana. When he was sent overseas, she returned to her mother in Brooklyn.

Although she missed my father, my mother was glad this part of her life was over. She frequently mentioned the prejudicial attitudes, Spartan accommodations, upstate cold and southern mud that she, a lifelong city dweller, had encountered in these duty stations. The only good thing, she related, was that since my father was head of the officer's mess, she always had plenty to eat, in spite of wartime rationing.

When the war ended, like everyone else, the two of them began making up for lost time. So I, along with many others, became part of the "baby boom"—that acceleration in birthrate that is a common occurrence after wartime. My father and his twin brother bought the bakery, my mother toiled there along with her Italian in-laws, and everyone seemed to adjust. Although it was not all smooth—Gerry experienced continuing tensions with her mother-in-law and to the end felt like a perpetual outsider—by the time I came along, the remaining tensions were shoved below the surface.

My parents hung on the words of the local pharmacist, the most respected man in our neighborhood, one of the few with any higher education. They often quoted him since he had assured my parents that mixed marriages were good, producing intelligent and beautiful children. My parents were especially pleased at my appearance when I was born. They took great satisfaction that I looked like a *real* American. For I was thin, had curly, auburn hair, light skin, freckles, a small nose, and blue eyes. Before I was even old enough to talk, they were already predicting that someday I might enter the Miss America pageant in nearby Atlantic City.

This focus on WASP (White Anglo-Saxon Protestants) attributes may seem a shame from our perspective today, which recognizes a range of racial and ethnic beauty standards. But at the time, the white Anglo-Saxon look was the "gold standard," and the closer one got to it, the more likely the child would find acceptance in the wider society. It may seem unfortunate that my parents especially valued my *"anglo"* appearance, but that's the way it was. Except for my Italian name, I didn't really stand out. Was I set up, early on, by my parents to want to "pass" in WASP culture?

These are not things I ever discussed with my parents, for they were busy with other, more practical things: the bakery and raising a family. My mother was simply relieved that she had married a "good provider" and was willing to work hard in the bakery. She learned some basic Italian and how to make "gravy," *pasta y fagioli*, escarole and beans, and my father's other favorites. Six years after I was born, she gave birth to a son and they named him Eugene, an anglicized version of my father's Italian name, Egidio.

My father focused on pastry and on keeping his wife happy. He worked hard, twelve hours a day, and came upstairs exhausted, often falling asleep in front of the television. But at least once a week, he would take my mother out to eat, into New York to eat a corned-beef sandwich at Lindy's, or to visit her mother in Brooklyn. He was generous to a fault, believed in taking vacations, and tried to keep the family calm and content. He hated strife of any kind and often served as a peacemaker in family conflicts.

One thing that neither of them ever did, however, was to practice or even mention religion. Once my father married, although he had once been an altar boy in Italy, he never again attended mass. I never saw him pray, cross himself, or own any kind of religious icon. Likewise, my mother did not observe the Jewish holidays, attend synagogue, or search for other Jews in the area to connect with. Still, she never gave up her religious identity. Conversion to Catholicism was out of the question. In fact, conversion to anything, as far as I know, never even occurred to either of them. My father would not have dreamed of becoming Jewish. Although he didn't practice his religion, he believed that "once a Catholic, always a Catholic," something that went double for an Italian Catholic.

Today there are many mixed-faith partnerships and their arrangements vary widely from practicing both, to only one, to none at all. But if anyone ever asks me, I contend that the worst solution of all is to allow a religious vacuum to exist. For children are naturally spiritual and, if not hindered, will easily believe in God. To have no guidance is difficult for a child, especially when one's friends and other relatives have a faith identity. But worst of all is to keep one's home a religious "no man's land," a tense place where the natural human questions about spiritual meaning and values are not allowed expression.

In my parents' day, few people claimed to be non-religious and no one said, as they do today, that they were "spiritual but not religious." Yet even though my parents never disavowed their backgrounds, they were not spiritual seekers. They seemed to prefer to keep religion on a back shelf like a wedding gift they felt too guilty to get rid of. Their religions were not discarded, but they were not displayed either. They would never have considered choosing a new faith that both could subscribe to, especially not Protestantism.

Protestants and Other Outsiders

We did have some Protestants in our neighborhood, although not many. There was a black Baptist church on the corner of Bloomfield and Clifton. Each Sunday morning families milled around outside before and after the service. They were always dressed up in a way that demonstrated that Sunday church was something really important to them. I envied their family togetherness and the way they seemed happy to be there.

The white Protestants, or *real "Medicans,"* as Grandma Angela called them, lived in the ritzy Forest Hills section just a few blocks behind Bloomfield Avenue. Their churches were formidable brick and stone structures. I knew nothing about the people who attended, didn't understand that there were different denominations, and never saw them milling outside like the black Baptists. Although I didn't know any of these Protestants, I thought of them as the *real* white people. I imagined they must be very quiet, very clean, very thin, and very well dressed in dark colors and expensive fabrics, kind of like the models I saw in *The New York Times* ads.

The little information I got about Protestants came from my family, for if there was one thing all my relatives agreed on completely, it was Protestants. My cousins—who seemed to be more religiously "in the know" than I was—warned me that if I even so much as put a foot into a Protestant church, I'd go straight to hell. My Jewish relatives preferred not to talk about Protestants at all, but it was clear that they lumped them in with other Jew-killers. My mother went further and regarded Protestants as more dangerous than Catholics.

Both my parents were clear about the Protestant profile, and they tried to fill me in: Protestants were cold and unfriendly. They were stingy; their food was terrible and they were prejudiced against Jews, Italians, Catholics, and anyone else that didn't arrive on the *Mayflower*. My father noted they didn't even appreciate that "it was an Italian, for chrissake, who discovered America." Protestants didn't even know how to relate to people or make them feel welcome. This was clinched for Gerry the one time she was invited to a Protestant's house. For years, my mother would relate the story:

"We came in, sat on the sofa, and she gave us some juice in little glasses. That's it. Then we went into the dining room and sat down. There was no food on the table. The woman actually went into the kitchen and made up the plates there," she said, her voice rising at this point in the story with horror and shock. "Each plate had on it only a spoonful of peas and a little piece of meatloaf! We couldn't get any more food than that."

My mother would then sit back with a look of satisfaction, sure her point had been made. I always felt a little chill when she told this incident, picturing dark, colorless rooms and gray-faced, gaunt, unsmiling people. My father always nodded his head seriously throughout the story. Often he would add a warning that I not expect too much from people of English, German, French, or any other descent linked to Protestantism. In fact, whenever I would talk about someone I knew, he would insist on knowing their last name.

"Hmmm, Hartsfield, what kind of name is that, Gerry? German? English? Or is that maybe one of your *lantsman*?"— in other words, a fellow Jew.

Together they would puzzle it out, trying to give me some indication of what to expect, based on the person's possible ethnic origin. My family was not so different from other immigrant and marginalized people who find comfort in the familiarity of the biologically related and the similar. In the face of the dominant culture, they felt insecure, expecting censure and rejection. So, as with the enculturation of a black child, my parents were determined to show me how to anticipate and preferably avoid the discrimination they had encountered.

Although my parents were very hospitable, it was clear to me that having "strangers" in our home—people not like us, not Italian and not Jewish—made my parents nervous. On the infrequent occasions when we would have a non-family member visit us, such as friends of my brother's or mine, they insisted on making a special meal. Even though I might beg them not to worry so much, I knew it was futile for me to try to stop their special preparations. It would be unheard of not to entertain a stranger. But it made me sick at heart to see my parents so tense and concerned.

"What if they don't like Italian food?" my father would keep asking before they arrived, with some anguish in his voice. "Don't use too much garlic, Gerry," he would caution. "Maybe we should just have steak and forget the spaghetti."

My mother would try to reassure him and also make sure we had enough variety to accommodate different tastes, but I could tell she was worried, too. In the end, our friends would always rave about the hospitality and generosity of my parents—and the fabulous desserts straight from our bakery. Still, I always thought a long time before inviting a friend over, and I instinctively restricted my invitations to Italian Catholic or Jewish friends. When I was growing up, not even one Protestant came through our apartment door. I had no way of knowing how much this would change just a few years later.

Chapter Two

The Little Jewish Girl Who Wanted a Crucifix, Too

My mother was not completely happy living and working in the North Ward. She always complained of being exhausted by the bakery and often seemed vaguely resentful. Over time, I gathered from her attitude that certain things were just not right in Newark.

One hot summer day when I was about five, my mother took me into the soda fountain about a block from our store. The place was cool and dark, and the man behind the counter smiled as I jumped up on one of his high stools covered in a dark red plastic.

"I'll have a Black Cow," my mother said with assurance.

"A Black Cow? What's that, Mommy?" I asked in a shocked whisper. I'd never seen any cows at all in Newark, and no black ones even in pictures, but the man knew just what she wanted.

"Oh, you'll see. It's delicious. I drank them all the time in New York," she said, sounding important.

"They also call them Black and Whites," the man said over his shoulder as he hit the palm of his hand two times hard on the top of a metal pump connected to a large silver container. Out came some thick dark brown stuff into the tall glass. Next he put in some milk and then got a big silver bottle and squirted something bubbly into the drink.

"We call that seltzer in New York," my mother said to me, low so the man couldn't hear. "That's the real name. Here they call it club soda."

The drink was delicious, but they both just laughed when I asked where the cow was. One thing I did understand, though, was that Newark had nothing on New York. My mother, who had lived all her life in the metropolitan area, clearly considered New Jersey a step down. One of the problems, I later realized, was that my mother missed being with Jews.

As far as I could tell, virtually no Jews lived in the North Ward. Although Newark did have a "Jewish section," Weequahic, which housed several prominent synagogues, we never went there. Instead, on my parents' day off, we would often visit her old locales, Brooklyn, the Bronx, and Coney Island. In these places, and especially when we visited her family, my mother seemed much more animated and relaxed. Also, at her insistence, we always spent our spring vacation in Miami at a hotel that catered to a Jewish clientele.

"Nu . . . this is your daughter, Gerry?" one of my mother's bingo partners would invariably ask, with the singsong quality I had come to associate with Jewish people. Tipping up my face with her hand, she'd scrutinize me and say, "So, she doesn't look Jewish." But another friend would look closely at me and insist, "Of course she does, look at her hair and her eyes." My father always seemed embarrassed and uncomfortable at these exchanges, no matter which way the assessment went.

At the hotel, I tried to share my mother's enthusiasm for pickled herring and chopped liver but felt confused when my father said a low "ooooh" under his breath and passed up these standard appetizers in favor of tomato juice. Each Friday in the hotel they served a bread that my mother called "holly."

"This is Jewish," she'd say portentously, and I felt that this sweet, yellowish, braided loaf must have some mysterious meaning, which I was expected to automatically understand. It wasn't until college that my Jewish roommate explained to me this was "challah," a special egg bread for the Sabbath. Mostly for my mother's benefit, we would often ride into Manhattan on the bus, arrive at Port Authority and then hail a cab. Invariably, my father would tell the cab driver, almost apologetically: "We're from Jersey." I cringed every time he gave away our real and clearly inferior identities. I didn't feel any better when, just as regularly, my mother would add emphatically "No, *I'm* from New York."

And just like clockwork, my mother would invariably ask the driver to drop us off at Lindy's, the large, crowded deli in midtown that my mother used to frequent when she was single. We would each order a huge corned-beef sandwich with mustard on rye, and, while we were waiting, my mother would help herself with obvious satisfaction to the open bowl of kosher pickles on the table. My father would eye the communal pickles with concern, each time asking, "Why do they use so much garlic?" When our sandwiches arrived, I could never fit mine into my mouth, much less finish it. Sometimes, if her purse was a large one, my mother would carefully wrap up my leftovers and take it with us "for later."

Then we would go to the lavishly decorated Radio City Music Hall for a movie and the Rockettes show. I followed the dancers' routines with rapt attention, feeling sure my life would be perfect if only I could be one of them. Afterwards we would grab a cup of coffee and a doughnut at Chock Full o' Nuts, then walk down 42nd Street on our way back to Port Authority. In New York, my mother acted happier and more relaxed than she ever did in Newark. Here my father deferred to her superior knowledge of city ways, and she suddenly became more confident, sophisticated, knowledgeable, and worldly.

Life in the North Ward had been an adjustment for my mother. Nevertheless, because she loved my father, she also grew to like many aspects of Italian culture and food. She developed a small repertoire of Italian dishes, admired Italian jewelry and leather goods, and eventually made several trips to Italy, which she raved about. She tried to share my father's enjoyment of opera and acted proud when he insisted we were related to the famous Italian composer Giuseppe Saverio Raffaele Mercadante. And although everyone else in the family grew sick of our pastries, she never did. My father teased her by saying she ate them when no one was looking. To pay for her sins, she would sporadically attend Weight Watchers.

But there was one thing about living in the North Ward that positively repulsed my mother: our neighborhood's religiosity. She would sometimes say, with a little shiver of disgust, that all the statues and especially the crucifixes "gave her the creeps." Her discomfort was especially evident when we had to attend a funeral or wedding in Sacred Heart Cathedral. It was hard to sit next to her at those events. For she held herself rigid, aloof, and very quiet as though merely breathing the church air might jeopardize her in some way. Often after these events, my mother spoke darkly of the anti-Semitism she felt was everywhere under the surface of Christianity.

She didn't have to go far to find it. Grandma Angela was prejudiced against nearly everyone who wasn't Italian and Catholic. The old señora never tried to hide this and frequently was rude to my mother, throwing out curses in Italian, which no one would translate for me. Although my mother tried to accommodate Grandma Angela—her eating preferences, her favored chair, her television shows—the older woman never seemed satisfied. I guess, by her lights, people that wouldn't end up in heaven with her didn't warrant any consideration.

Grandma Angela didn't seem to like me, either, since I was the first fruit of this mixed union. Perhaps my parents tried to mollify her by naming me Linda Angela, but it didn't help. Grandma was from the "old school." She was easily annoyed, quick with a slap, and expected children to generally stay out of the way.

At dinner, which she often ate in our apartment, I sat across from her at the small Formica table in our kitchen. At the start of every meal, she would remove her false teeth and place them in front of my plate. When she was full, she would lean back and push her dirty plate forward, until it collided with mine.

"Daddy, why does she always have to do that?" I would whine, feeling offended and disgusted. But my father invariably shushed me, making it known that Grandma Angela's ways would have to be tolerated.

Grandma Angela was especially touchy during her favorite television show, *Life Is Worth Living*, with Bishop Fulton J. Sheen. Even though she didn't understand a word, she would watch the ornately dressed cleric with rapt attention, occasionally praising him by saying, *"Quanto si bello"*—how beautiful!

One time I passed between her and the television set during this show, on my way to the bathroom. She jumped up, screamed something in Italian, and began to flail at me with nails out like a tiger. Seeing her coming at my face, hands claw-like, petrified me, and I raised my arms in defense. Besides the scratches, I was accused of the most heinous crime, "fighting with your grandmother." Complaining about these things never did any good. Someone would always say in a shocked tone: "She's your grandmother! You have to respect her."

I was afraid of Grandma and was much more comfortable when she was upstairs in her own apartment. Although eventually I learned to understand some of what she said, I never had a real conversation with her. As part of her dislike of America, she refused to learn English. And no one thought it necessary to teach the grandchildren Italian, for we were to be "real Americans." Even with the language barrier, however, Grandma Angela was a very large presence in my life. She ate with us, always vacationed with us at the Jersey shore, and spent most of her day in the bakery. As she got older she even began staying overnight with us in our small apartment. My little brother's room was the only one with any extra space, so he was relegated to a cot, while she got his bed. That was the only time I was grateful that my room was much smaller than his.

To be honest, Grandma Angela wasn't too grandmotherly toward any of her grandchildren. I observed this firsthand in the summer when my father, his twin, and their sister shared a rented vacation house, usually in Belmar, at the Jersey shore. The five kids got to stay for the entire season, while the parents went back and forth. They took turns staffing the shop back in the city during the quieter summer months when business was slower. As usual, during what I came to think of as "the changing of the guard," we were left alone with Grandma Angela while one couple drove to Newark to relieve the other couple.

On these changing days, Grandma insisted we stay in the house with her, rather than going to the beach, as we did every other day. Being at the shore was like the "Fresh Air Fund" for my cousins and me. We all loved playing in the waves, walking on the jetty, visiting the food stands and arcades. We'd walk there as a family, loaded down with towels, blankets, an umbrella, sandwiches, and we'd stay all day. I hated to miss even one minute and would look forward to these two months all year long.

But there was no changing Grandma's mind. Perhaps she

was afraid she'd lose us if she took us to the beach. On one of these changing days, around two o'clock, Grandma decided we should all eat. She called my brother, my two cousins, and me to the large table in the dining room, giving us each a bowl of *pasta e fagioli* and an empty juice glass. After saying something in Italian, Grandma went into a closet and brought out a large open bottle of ginger ale.

"Wow," I thought with amazement. "She's going to give us some of her ginger ale. Maybe she's getting nicer." Grandma Angela loved ginger ale. At mealtime she always kept a large bottle of it on the floor right next to her chair. If you even got near it, she would push you away, then put her hands over it, and say something in Italian dialect that sounded like "*Geesio me.*" We knew this meant "This is mine."

But today was going to be different, I thought, as a warm feeling spread over me. As Grandma started pouring the ginger ale into our glasses, I noticed right away that there were no bubbles in it.

"*Hmmm, it's flat. Why do we have to get it when it's flat?*" I thought with some resentment. But then I noticed that there was also something floating in it. "Yuk!" I exclaimed loudly to the other kids, "there's *ants* in it!"

"Oh, gross," said one cousin.

"How disgusting," said another. "She's just giving us her old stuff."

We never cared what we said to each other in English, because we were sure Grandma couldn't understand us. Still, we knew we had to finish everything. Grandma was strong, and she was quick. We all knew that if we annoyed her she might come at us with a frying pan, a broom, a pot of boiling water, or her hand. While I was usually angry or afraid, the other kids seemed to think it was funny.

Ironically, however, Grandma Angela was also the most religious person I knew. I was very impressed with her public devotions. Every day she positioned herself at the red Formica table near the front door of our shop right next to the display window. There she would pray her rosary beads, read from a prayer book, or look at her holy cards. Unlike the other women of her generation, who dressed in somber black, my grandmother often wore floral silks, so she really stood out.

Since I always left and returned through the store, rather than our apartment, I passed her at her post many times a day. She would rarely disturb her devotions to look up at me. Her religion created a wall around her. If I ever got too close as she sat by the window or if I tried to touch her religious objects, she would push me away.

Given this disjunction between her behavior and her religiosity, I developed a real ambivalence toward outward displays of piety. Still, I desperately wanted some religion in my life, and Grandma Angela would have been the logical family member to address this need. Perhaps at one time she had tried. For my mother revealed with bitterness that, when I was an infant, my grandmother had tried to get me baptized. She had hidden me in a blanket, had left the bakery with me, and was walking fast toward the church when my mother saw her through the shop window, ran outside, and intercepted her. Grandma Angela must have dismissed me as lost after that.

A Misfit

My grandmother's treatment of me may have been extreme, but my other relatives and friends had a similar assessment. According to the other children, I was "nothing." To the adults, I was an object of pity or disdain. Even the few Protestants at school judged me similarly. For although

Protestants and Catholics did not mix well in that day, the one thing they *did* agree upon was that an unbaptized person like myself was going to end up in hell. Although the Jews I knew did not worry about hell, they were also concerned about my identity. I was told that, with a Jewish mother, I was Jewish, but no one really treated me that way. My status seemed questionable, what with my Italian last name and Catholic father. No effort was made to educate me in Judaism, teach me how to celebrate the holidays, or take me to synagogue. I sensed that I would never be "really" Jewish, would never fully measure up no matter what. Especially when we were among Jews unrelated to me, I sensed a visceral hesitancy.

Even when I was with my warm and loving Jewish relatives, I often felt sadness and longing. On our visits, they would good-naturedly tease my reserved and quiet father, who appeared to feel so obviously out of place in the "alien" environment of New York. And his uneasiness spread to me. Although I envied my Jewish relatives' large circle of friends and strong sense of identity, I knew deep down that I could never fit into their world.

Jungian psychologists say that every person carries some primal "wound" throughout life. I know now that, for me, it was this lack of a clear identity and a group to which I really belonged. I wasn't "really" Italian, I wasn't "really" Jewish, I wasn't really anything. But, according to most people, I would be carrying my wound into the next life, too—where I would land in hell. For some reason that was not explained, I would not even win the consolation prize of limbo, which is where Catholics said little unbaptized babies went who died at birth.

Although, like the Virgin, I "pondered these things in my heart," I did not feel free to voice these feelings anywhere, to anyone. In our home the topic of religion was not allowed, and even seemed shameful. I became terribly afraid of exposing myself to others. Why would anyone want to befriend someone who was headed straight for hell? But it took a lot of emotional energy to keep this misbegotten inner self camouflaged. I became very attentive to cultural differences, trying hard—not always successfully—to "blend in" no matter who I was with. Everywhere I went I felt like a misfit, a pretender, or an object of pity.

In school, the pledge of allegiance, prayer, and Bible reading were conducted each morning. I would keep my eyes slightly open so I could see how the Catholics folded their hands and made the sign of the cross. When we recited the Lord's Prayer, I followed just a syllable behind. For some reason that I never understood, all the Catholics would stop at "deliver us from evil," while the few lone Protestants would continue on. The times I got carried away and kept going proved conclusively to the Catholic children that, no matter what my last name, I was not one of them.

Most of all, I learned to never mention my mother's religion. From early on I had heard enough ugly anti-Semitic remarks to make me worried. People spoke of Jews as being cheap, or loud, or the ones who killed Christ. Even one of my own cousins blithely commented that he could "jew" someone down on a price. I was confused and ashamed when I heard these remarks, but I rarely said anything. Worse, I was terrified when I heard adults talk about what Hitler had done to the Jews. It seemed dangerous simply to *be* Jewish.

I couldn't stand living like this. I didn't want to go to hell. I didn't want to be persecuted. I needed an identity— but a safe identity. In my childish mind, maybe if I had a cross, some statues . . . then, I would be protected, I would be "something," and maybe God would notice me.

Sleeping Above the Tavern

Something else added to my anxiety about identity: the "mainstream America" I saw on television. Shows like *Father Knows Best* or *Leave It to Beaver* showed quiet streets, lovely houses, large lawns, dressed-up mothers in their own kitchens, and fathers who went out every morning to an office wearing freshly pressed suits and neatly knotted ties.

Not all the ways my family differed from these television families seemed bad, of course. I liked having family around all the time, and I was proud of my parents' expertise and our business's good reputation. But I resented the long hours and constant attention they devoted to the bakery. And why did we have to live above the business on noisy, dirty Bloomfield Avenue? Why did we have to endure the roaches that brazenly roamed our apartment at all hours, impossible to control because of the bakery downstairs? Why did Grandma have to remove her false teeth at dinner and blithely place them on the table? Why did we have to own a business that made our clothes stained and dirty so much of the time? This wasn't the kind of place I could confidently bring friends whose own families lived on quiet streets in real houses, with backyards, tablecloths, and clean clothes. It was just easier to play with my cousins.

Our apartment only had two bedrooms, so when my brother was born, my parents took a tiny alcove off the living room and made it into a small bedroom for me, just large enough for a twin bed, small dresser, and chair. I was six now, they said, and old enough to have my own bedroom in the front of the apartment. They said it was a big privilege to have this special new room, and I tried to appreciate it. But my window looked right out on Bloomfield Avenue, where large trucks rumbled by at all hours, spewing diesel exhaust and making my bed shake. Below was a tavern, where loud voices and music would wake me up. And occasionally there would be burglary attempts on the stores below. I lived in panic that they would come upstairs and find me first. I felt more exposed than the other family members who had bedrooms in the back of the three apartments.

It didn't help that this was the Cold War era, with air-raid drills in school, television shows about nuclear war, and government recommendations for building a bomb shelter in your basement. Our apartment seemed more vulnerable than a house. For a time I kept a doll-size suitcase at the foot of my bed, stocked with underwear and cookies. When I suggested we build a bomb shelter below the bakery, my father laughed.

"Don't worry. We could just go into the store's basement. We have lots of food down there."

Picturing us surviving in that dark, damp, and dirty place, with the roaches and mice, made me feel even more scared. I was sure that if we lived in a house in a real neighborhood everything would be better. When I got old enough, I began to spend hours walking or riding my bike in nearby Forest Hills. The large, beautiful homes there seemed to promise peace, tranquility, and love. I dreamed of having my family greet me at the door, in a clean house with no bakery smell, no custard cream clinging to everyone's clothes, no cramped rooms, and no workaday atmosphere. I would look out my window on quiet streets, trees, and grass.

The closest to this in my family was Aunt Mary's home. It was within walking distance of the bakery, and I visited there as often as I could. Although Aunt Mary's family lived in a lower-middle-class neighborhood of small frame houses, much less impressive than Forest Hills, their home looked like a palace to me. It was a real house with two floors, a finished basement, a backyard, and even a dog. My cousin Dorothy, an only child, seemed so lucky. She had her own bedroom upstairs and another room for her desk and toys. No loud traffic disturbed their tranquility. Kids could actually play in the street, and my cousin just had to cross it to get to her best friend's house.

Besides being the best cook in our extended family, my aunt dressed beautifully, doted on her daughter, and was nice to me, too. I saw her every day, since she worked in our business. When I developed a rash from unlined wool pants and my mother would not buy me the more expensive lined ones, my aunt quietly presented me with a pair, which I wore until they were almost in shreds. I was drawn to this family but couldn't understand why. Since they were Italian, like us, and worked in the same bakery business, I figured it must be the house that made them more confident and comfortable with who they were.

"Why can't we just get a house like Aunt Mary's?" I would often ask my parents. "You could still get to the store. She does it."

"No, stop asking, we can't do that. We have to be near the business," they would always say, angry at my persistence and impracticality.

But I was convinced that a house would keep us safer, help us fit in better, allow me to have friends visit, and make everything all right. My parents were unresponsive to my pleas, and I couldn't articulate the depth of my fears and longings to them or even to myself. All I knew was that despite the warmth and security of my little Italian world, I continued to feel afraid, misplaced, and misbegotten. Perhaps that's why I eventually began to take matters into my own hands.

The Prize

One day I attended a cousin's birthday party. Not usually good at games, I was amazed when I won at pin-the-tail-on-the-donkey. I felt even better—in fact, overjoyed and elated—when I unwrapped the game prize. Inside the little white box I found a tiny gold crucifix sitting on a small fluffy cotton square. It looked more beautiful than anything I had ever seen. And it was mine. When I got home, I didn't show my treasure to anyone but quietly went into the kitchen, got a piece of twine, and threaded it through. After my parents tucked me in that night, I got up and put it on. At last I had my very own cross, and now I looked like "something" to the world, even if I wasn't yet sure what that "something" was. At least now God might notice me, and I might get some of that special power inside.

I slept late and woke up the next morning to *Captain Kangaroo* on the television outside my bedroom door. My mother had propped up my baby brother on the coffee table and was feeding him. As I came out of my bedroom and walked by them on my way to the kitchen, my mother caught sight of me, grabbed my shoulder, and pulled me over to her. With a quick, rough jerk, she ripped the little crucifix off my neck. As I stared at her in shock, feeling the place where the twine had cut into my neck, she said in clipped and angry tones: "Little Jewish girls don't wear crosses."

My mother's violent reaction might have been enough to scare me away from religion, but my need was too great. I continued to quietly covet religious jewelry and statuary. I showed interest when my Italian relatives attended church, hoping they would invite me along. When they did, I was awed and impressed by the mass. And anytime I was given any money, I furtively used it to buy my own religious objects. After smuggling them into the apartment, I would hide them around my room like a teenage boy with pornographic magazines. At the same time, though, I would feel guilty and conflicted, vaguely aware that what seemed to make me so happy might also be disloyal or even wrong.

Soon after the cross incident, Angela, my favorite cousin and, at seven, just a year younger, began attending classes to make her first communion. Like me, she went to public school, and catechism for public school children was held on Sunday morning. At mass in the cathedral beforehand, the children got to sit in a special pew, with black-habited nuns who clapped once for the children to kneel, twice for them to stand, and once again for them to file out and over to the classroom building.

Their unity and sense of purpose really appealed to me. And the cathedral, which I had always admired from the outside, was even more wonderful inside. Its gorgeous stained-glass windows, marble carvings, and stunning acoustics for the weekly Gregorian chant all created a world very different from our grimy, noisy one just two blocks away. So I begged to attend catechism with my cousin and, amazingly, was allowed to go. Perhaps it was seen simply as a couple of hours of free childcare and a way to get me out from underfoot on Sunday mornings, a very busy time in the shop.

If my parents could have seen ahead, they probably wouldn't have let me go. The classes felt like a great feast after a long famine. At last I heard about what was true, right, and good, and I heard about my place in the scheme of things. There was a dark side as well, however. For in pre–Vatican II Catholicism, all teaching included a heavy dose of rules and admonitions. Questions were discouraged, even seen as sinful, and hell was a key topic. I learned that no one but Catholics would go to heaven. "*So,*" I realized, "*my Catholic friends have been right all along.*"

In the Baltimore Catechism, I read a disturbing confirmation of the dismissal of Judaism that I had been detecting all along:

391. Why did the Jewish religion, which up to the death of Christ had been the true religion, cease at that time to be the true religion?

A. The Jewish religion, which, up to the death of
Christ, had been the true religion, ceased at that time
to be the true religion, because it was only a promise
of the redemption and figure of the Christian religion, and when the redemption was accomplished
and the Christian religion established by the death
of Christ, the promise and the figure were no longer
necessary.

So my mother's religion was no longer true, and my father was in mortal sin for not attending mass. I couldn't
allow myself to think too much about the eternal fate of either one. Finally I got up the nerve to ask my father about
this. Like a lot of Italian Catholics, especially the men, he
didn't place his trust in church authority.

"Oh, don't worry about that," my father said, reassuringly.
"God will take anyone who is leading a good life."

That sounded nice, but with my half-and-half background,
I didn't feel I could afford to take any chances. Still, fear
wasn't my whole motivation for attending the class. I wanted
to know how to be good, I wanted to belong somewhere, and
most important, I simply liked catechism and mass. Even
with all the rules and warnings, it was so satisfying to hear
someone speak of God openly. The experience filled me with
hope and a deep inexplicable joy. I would get a little shiver
of delight every time we said "Holy, Holy, Holy, Lord God
Almighty, Heaven and earth are full of your glory. Hosanna
in the highest. Blessed is He who comes in the name of the
Lord. Hosanna in the highest." The words seemed tinged
with gold.

But catechism class was not without its dangers. For one
day toward the middle of the year, the nun pulled me aside.

"Linda, you can't receive your first communion unless
you're baptized. I'm going to send a priest to your home to

tell your parents. I'm sure your father will understand," she said patronizingly.

I was devastated. I didn't know how she had learned of my background. I had never mentioned it. But when I got home and timidly broached this information, my mother was incensed. She got on the phone and insisted the priest not be sent to our home. Then there were angry words between my parents behind closed doors. Hearing them argue filled me with dread. One evening, after another such argument between them, my mother exited their bedroom, passed me, and said bitterly, "If your father and I get a divorce, it will be your fault."

The arguments between my parents eventually stopped. Perhaps my mother felt she had no chance of opposing me in such a Catholic environment, or perhaps my father persuaded her to let me do what I wanted. All I knew was that her discouragements went underground, forming into a root of bitterness.

Meanwhile, I had a new spiritual quandary. I had learned in catechism that if one's parents were not married in the church, they were not truly married in the eyes of God, which meant that children of this union were not legitimate. I seemed to be getting further and further away from becoming Catholic. Fortunately, my Aunt Marie—who was not exactly a theologian—straightened it all out for me, but she did so in a way that I now realize was comically erroneous but also well intentioned, loving, even godly: "Well, Linda, you know that Jesus was Jewish . . . and he became Catholic."

Given my environment, the fact that Jesus was Catholic hardly surprised me, but I had never heard before that Jesus was also Jewish. When I heard this I relaxed. Surely he would know what I was feeling, and if he had done it, so could I. I began to feel a presence with me, protecting, reassuring, and giving me courage. So I carried on. I selected my own godparents, my father's sister and his twin brother, and a date was set for my baptism. One sunny spring afternoon, the three of us walked over to the cathedral, met with the priest, and it was accomplished.

I had converted. I was overjoyed that now I was a Catholic and part of the church. Now I was "something" and God was with me. Things were much clearer, because I finally had an identity. Inside I felt grounded and secure for the first time. Not only that, but the Baltimore Catechism, which we had to memorize, told me right up front what my purpose in life was. In fact, I have been feeding off the sixth question/ answer pair since the day I first read it:

6. Q. Why did God make you?

A. God made me to know Him, to love Him, and to serve Him in this world, and to be happy with Him forever in heaven.

The Perpetual Rift

I made my first communion and tagged along at the party my cousin's parents gave for her. My mother had been sending mixed—though predominantly negative—signals. She had allowed my aunt to order my special outfit—white lacy dress and veil, patent leather shoes, white gloves, and prayer book—along with Angela's. And she had made sure I got up on time for the event. But her disgust came out in a perpetually annoyed tone of voice. In fact, my guilt at angering my mother vied with my newfound sense of belonging. By choosing God, I felt I had chosen against her. So, although I was relieved to be a Catholic, my conversion put a permanent rift between us.

I did not learn until years later that my mother had in-sisted upon—and apparently received—a promise from my father that any children produced by their union would be raised Jewish. Would this knowledge have helped me relate better to my mother during my childhood struggles to es-tablish an identity? Probably not. But knowing it now does inform and color my memories of my mother's attempts to strengthen my connection to my Jewish roots—a campaign that began suddenly, soon after she discovered that I was wearing a crucifix. Before that incident, she had not made any effort to get me to identify with Judaism, but afterwards she began insisting that I watch old newsreels of Nazi con-centration camps, piles of dead bodies, and walking skele-tons being liberated by American soldiers.

"It doesn't matter that you have tried to become a Catholic," she said to me soon after my baptism. "Hitler would still put you in a concentration camp."

Her statement chilled me to the core, gave me night-mares, and haunted me for years. Yet I saw no other way out of my dilemma—and the appearance that I might be re-jecting her and my Jewish roots. What better place to turn, in the face of desperation, fear, and a lack of identity, but God? Of course, I was relieved that I would not be going to hell and that I had a religion at last, but it was more than that. The messages I had heard at mass, catechism, and in my cousin's prayer books—and even the church architec-ture, hymns, and trinkets I loved—had promised peace, joy, and identity. Not only that, but I felt sure Jesus knew what it was like to be a misfit. I knew that he could understand my fears. I was comforted by the fact that people did not understand him, and he came from a place no more highly regarded than Newark. A positive spiritual message and presence had drawn me into the church. I felt on God's side now, protected, loved, recognized. I had chosen *for* something, not *against*.

I had been taught in catechism that it was a mortal sin to miss mass, so from then on I made every effort to go each Sunday. I knew I would feel better if I went to church, but getting there was hard. No one was in our apartment—they were all working downstairs—so I had to get myself up on time and figure out what to wear. I never dressed up like the other kids I saw at church. For one thing, when I walked through the bakery, I would surely get dirty. And if I tried to leave through our apartment building's front door, instead, my mother would accuse me of sneaking out. For another, why should I celebrate something my mother obviously felt was wrong? It was bad enough that I insisted on going at all, I thought, so there was no point in flaunting it.

When there was no one to go to church with, which was often, I walked there alone, sat alone, and returned home alone. No one ever spoke to me during the service, and seeing the other children sitting there with parents and grandparents made me feel especially lonely.

Many of the homilies focused on the importance of having the whole family be regular in their devotions. An important slogan at the time was "The family that prays together, stays together." But I knew it was futile to hope I would ever have a real Catholic family who would go to church with me.

Perhaps this is why going to church has remained an ambivalent experience for me. Now, as then, I do not like going to church alone. As a child, I always felt isolated, small, and invisible. Yet then, as now, I knew I had a right to be there. Apart from the loneliness, it felt good to be at church, like a warm quilt wrapped around my heart. Although the mass was in Latin, I always carried a translation with me, and there was plenty to look at, hear, and smell. The cathedral was overwhelmingly beautiful, the Gregorian chants captivating, and the church had a holy fragrance of its own. I felt safe there, hidden in the secret places of God. I knew experientially what I would later learn intellectually:

> I will go before you, and make the crooked places straight: I will break in pieces the gates of brass, and cut asunder the bars of iron:
> I will give you the treasures of darkness, and hidden riches of secret places, that you may know that it is I, the LORD, the God of Israel, who calls you by your name. (Isaiah 45:2–3)

Three Strikes Against Me

It was a lot of trouble being a girl in the North Ward. We were expected to be modestly chaste, yet darkly sexy. We had to look pretty, not practical. Short frilly dresses, thin-soled tight shoes, fancy hair, and little purses that could hold nothing but a tissue and a few coins were our gold standard. I envied the boys, who could wear pants all the time—with lots of pockets—and shoes they could run in. In the intense summer heat, boys could discard their shirts, and it didn't matter if they wore the same sort of thing day after day.

Girls who wanted to be active were limited by more than just their clothes. While I had a bike and a jump rope, no other athletic equipment was considered proper. Girls were expected to spend most of their time playing house with dolls—interspersed with coloring—and helping their mothers. Those things were fine, but I longed for more. I especially wanted to be like the cowboys I saw on television. Once, as we passed a shoe store, I stopped to admire a beautiful pair of cowboy boots. My mother was horrified but wanted to teach me a lesson. So she took me inside, approached a salesman and asked confidently:

"You don't sell cowboy boots for girls, do you? They are only for boys, right?"

The salesman couldn't figure out which way my mother

wanted to go with this, so he hedged his bets. "Well, they do come in boys' sizes, but we can certainly try to fit her with a pair," he said.

As the man went off to get the foot-measuring device, my mother hustled me out of the store. "See," she said, "I told you these things aren't for girls."

It was good news when my mother had a baby boy. Soon, I knew, there would be better things to play with. As my brother got older, he didn't mind sharing his toys, but I was frustrated that I could only use these things—especially the sports equipment—at home with him. Unlike my brother, I could not join teams, wear uniforms, be coached, and have spectators cheer me. Male freedom didn't end with sports. When a boy entered his early teens, he got to roam the neighborhood with friends, hang out at the pizza parlor, have hours of unaccountable time, and come home well after dark—things girls were not allowed.

The whole thing drove me crazy. It wasn't fair, but no one could give me a good reason for these disparities in clothes, toys, and privilege. As a little girl, I didn't see that much difference between males and females, except for hair. For boys it was simple. They could choose between crew cuts or short, parted hair. They could swim without bathing caps and take a quick shower without worrying if they had time for hair-setting and drying. Girls' hair, on the other hand, caused problems and required effort. Before a girl was old enough for official "big" hair, she was expected to wear Shirley Temple curls, which took forever to fix. My frizzy, thick hair wouldn't stay in those curls for more than five minutes, and my mother constantly complained. She tried permanents, straightening lotions, and anything else she thought would tame my hair, but it seemed to have a mind of its own. The curl wars, with her shouting and me crying, happened all the time.

One day when I was about six, I got a marvelous idea. I was convinced it would easily take care of two problems at once, the curl wars and the restrictions that seemed attached to long hair. It was morning and all the adults were busy downstairs. No one saw me as I went up to our apartment. I knew my mother kept some half-rusty old metal scissors in the kitchen junk drawer. I got the scissors out, crawled under my bed, and started hacking at my imitation Shirley Temple curls. The scissors weren't very sharp, but I did the best I could. After cutting off the offending curls, I looked at myself in the mirror, more or less satisfied with the results.

I thought my mother wouldn't notice, or maybe she'd like the improved me. Soon I heard her coming upstairs. She called for me, and when I didn't come, she went into my room to find me sitting on the floor surrounded by strawberry blond hair.

"Hi, Mommy," I said, at first sort of proud and then sort of worried as I saw her face change from disinterest to rage.

"What in the world is the matter with you?" she screamed. This was getting to be her favorite question.

I couldn't really explain myself, but I mentioned something about boys having short hair. For some reason I could not fathom, this seemed to make her even angrier. She lifted me up by my remaining hair, saying:

"If you want to look like a boy, then I'm just going to take you to the barber and let him finish the job."

She grabbed my arm and dragged me outside. I knew I was in big trouble when we left—not through the bakery—but by the apartment's front door, reserved for weddings, funerals, and company. She hustled me across the street to the shop where my father got his hair cut. When the barber saw my mother's face, he took us right in. Although there were several old Italian men sitting in chairs along the wall waiting for their turn, they did not complain. Instead, they sized up the situation and stayed out of my mother's way, pointing and making low comments to each other.

"So you wanted short hair?" said the barber, amazingly nonchalant. With a few quick snips, he evened out my work. "Don't do it yourself next time," he said with a laugh as my mother paid him.

I liked the way I looked, and especially the way my head felt now, lighter and cooler. But I knew better than to mention this to my mother. If anything, she was even angrier, for the neighborhood would now know what I had done. I began to feel I had somehow inadvertently crossed a dangerous line.

"Wait until everyone sees you," my mother warned. "They already think you're crazy. Now they'll really know."

Suddenly, instead of free, I felt exposed and naked. As we crossed Bloomfield Avenue, I began to cry with shame and fear. Back in the bakery, my father hid his surprise and tried to assuage my upset with chuckling and kindly remarks. Even he, however, could not make my new, almost paralyzing dread go away.

I tried to toe the hair-line from then on. By my preteen years, I was wasting endless hours forcing my hair to pretend it was straight. Straight, big hair was the style, and it seemed no other girls in our neighborhood had unruly hair but me. It was especially difficult during summers at the Jersey shore, where the humid ocean air made my hair go absolutely wild. I would spend all afternoon with my hair set on big rollers, then carefully comb it out, tease it high, and shellac the result with hairspray. Then I would go outside and almost immediately begin to feel the horrible, tickly sensation of my bangs curling up on my forehead. Within minutes, the real, frizzy, unacceptable me was back.

It was only much later, when I began to study gender

issues, that I began to understand more about the female models of behavior that, at first, I rejected outright (my hair-cutting incident), then later tried so unsuccessfully to subscribe to (my elaborate struggles with frizzy hair). These gender behaviors and restrictions had been forced on me by my mother and the other women I knew just as those very same behaviors once had been forced on them. They surely feared, even if unconsciously, that their daughters would somehow stray outside acceptable bounds and be punished by society for it. I also realized later that males were not as free from restrictions as I once believed. Society dictated that males must keep their emotions in check, be strong all the time, and never inadvertently do something identified with females.

Yet females had two layers to negotiate. Not only were we prevented from stepping over into male territory, but we also had to negotiate the classic "virgin-whore" dichotomy, which both religion and culture foist on females. Actually, a clear-cut choice between virgin or whore would have been almost easy, but in my neighborhood and culture, something much more complicated was asked of females. We had to be as voluptuous as the worst possible bad girl, without actually being one—like the Italian national treasure, Sophia Loren. Simultaneously, we had to be not just a good girl, but the best girl ever—like the Virgin Mary.

Church Rubs It In

The Virgin Mary was a big deal in our neighborhood, with grottos and statues everywhere. I didn't hear much about her from family, but in church she was held up as the supreme role model for girls and women. Mother of God, perpetual virgin, submissive, pure, and holy—these were impossible goals. There were other ways, too, that the church confirmed my restricted female role. A female had to wear a modest dress to mass—never pants or, God forbid, shorts, and nothing sleeveless. Not only that, but we had to cover our heads with a veil or hat. If an absent-minded girl forgot to bring her head covering, she would stand in horror at the church door, sinful if she went in and sinful if she didn't. If she were lucky, someone would offer her a crumpled handkerchief or tissue, but then everyone would know of her disgraceful lapse.

There was never any explanation given, except "because you're a girl." At the time, I didn't realize that this head-covering issue came from 1 Corinthians 11:2–16, which states that "the head of every man is Christ, the head of a woman is her husband" (12:3) and that a man dishonors his head when it is covered during worship, but a woman's head is dishonored by being uncovered (12:4–5). The boiled-down version I was eventually given simply stated that women must wear something on their heads to show submission and that men take their hats off out of respect. It made no sense to me. The situation was confused even more by visits to my other, Jewish, world where men did just the opposite: they kept their hats or yarmulkes on during worship. Even as a child I think I realized that, for men, hats on and hats off both meant privilege.

This paradoxical situation from my childhood is, I think, what led me many years later to write my master's thesis and first book—*From Hierarchy to Equality: A Comparison of Past and Present Interpretations of 1 Cor. 11:2–16 in Relation to the Changing Status of Women in Society*. But a head covering was not the only restriction on lay females in the Catholic Church. For neither girls nor women were allowed behind the altar—except for nuns, sometimes, and then only to clean. Altar boys were . . . boys. Only they could have the up-front job that allowed them to wear the long, white alb, light the candles, hold the Bible, and load the censer with incense. Only they could stand behind the communion rail, holding the paten under people's chins, as the priest gave out communion. Altar boys seemed to have real, personal relationships with the usually austere and remote priests. Around these boys, the priests seemed almost relaxed, sharing a few words or even a laugh after mass. I was impressed that one of my younger cousins, Pat Junior, who lived in nearby Nutley and attended parochial school, was chosen to be an altar boy. I knew that his parents even had the priest over to dinner sometimes. One time Junior showed me that there were pictures of angels on nearly every page of his schoolbooks. This was all so beyond my own experience that I thought this family must be on a higher spiritual realm than ours. Plus, they lived in a real house, brick, with three floors, a lawn, and a park as their backyard. It seemed these things must be connected. If I visited and played with him as much as possible, maybe some of the holiness would rub off on me.

I longed to live in a house, to attend Catholic school, and to have religious books of my own. However, when I took a chance and asked my mother if I could go to parochial school, she seemed so horrified that I dropped the subject immediately. Yet even with all my repressed religiosity, I never considered becoming a nun. My Italian family would have done their best to discourage a religious vocation in any of us children. My relatives considered the religious life a sad state, separated as it was from what really mattered— family. To us cousins, nuns seemed austere and strict; priests seemed distant, slightly frightening, or at best, patronizing. Still, we were in awe of the "religious." After all, these people, especially priests, were the nearest thing to God.

My family was not unusual in their attitudes. Many Italian-American immigrants had ambivalent attitudes toward nuns and priests, and the church in general. For one thing, American priests were often of Irish descent, even in Italian immigrant parishes. These priests were often judgmental about what they perceived as the superstitious and less serious attitudes of Italian Catholics, with their adoration of saints and preference for the lavish *festa* rather than more institutional expressions of faith. Italian anti-clerical attitudes predated immigration, however, having been nurtured in Italy, where many considered the church hierarchy to be aligned with the wealthy landowners and shifting governmental alliances, rather than the poor, landless peasants.

Even though my Catholic relatives shared this ambivalent attitude toward the church, I could not afford any ambivalence. Given my mixed background and the fact that I usually went to church alone, I always felt at a severe spiritual disadvantage, which meant that I had to follow all the rules scrupulously and get everything perfect. If the church held the key to salvation, as they said they did, then I could not take a chance on accidentally disobeying their rules. For some reason, being on God's good side held a high importance for me.

But I didn't always get it right. One Saturday afternoon, at about age nine, preparing to enter the church for confession, I realized I had brought nothing for my head. But if I didn't go to confession, I could not receive communion at mass the next day. That meant one less bit of grace, one less indulgence. I couldn't afford that—I needed all the help I could get.

Feeling hopeless, I stood immobilized at the cathedral door. With no purse and no pockets in my clothes, I didn't even have my own tissue. As my eyes filled with tears of hopelessness, I didn't realize I was blocking a priest dressed in a long, black cassock, on his way to hear confessions. At first he tried to pass me but then looked down and asked what the problem was. When I explained, he laid his big warm hand on the top of my head for several moments, then lifted it off and said importantly:

"There. Now you have a hat."

"Are you sure I can go in like this, Father?" I asked incredulously.

He assured me that I could, and so I timidly entered, trying to keep an even lower profile than usual. I might be acceptable to him now, and maybe even to God, but what about the ushers and the old Italian ladies? They would still eye me with disgust and see the truth I always tried to hide, that I was an incompetent pretender, someone who did not come from a Catholic home.

A nun passed me as I walked down the aisle toward the confessionals. Eyeing my head, she frowned and gave out a little gasp. As I tried to walk by quickly and get into a confessional booth, where I would be hidden, she grabbed me by the shoulder and whispered, "Where's your hat, young lady?"

"Father said I didn't need it," I answered breathlessly. She gave me a disbelieving stare as I looked in vain for the priest.

"Really, he did. I forgot," I squeaked out. The nun looked disgusted, but produced a crumpled tissue from out of her voluminous black sleeve, clamped it to my head, and stomped away. Even at church, then, the one place where I really tried to follow all the rules, I could not measure up.

The Protocols of Being a Girl

My Jewish mother did not care about church protocols, of course, but she nevertheless became more concerned with my girl-ness as I entered my preteen years. When I was twelve, she announced one night at dinner: "Bamberger's has a 'Charm School' for girls. I'm going to enroll you in it.

It's on Saturday mornings for four weeks, and you can take the bus there."

Now I was allowed to travel alone downtown to the department store, dressed in my best outfit, nylons, and first pair of heels. A little beige leather purse dangled from my arm and I carried an umbrella just in case. My parents cautioned me to only sit next to women if the bus were crowded, gave me enough money get there and back, clear directions about which bus to take home, and sent me off. I crossed Bloomfield Avenue to get the downtown bus. Once aboard, I swayed a little as I walked down the aisle in the new dress shoes with the little beginners' high heel, but I felt very grown-up. Maybe things would change now.

I entered Bamberger's through the big glass doors. My mother and I had come here often, so I knew my way around. I took the escalator upstairs and found the designated room. Although my mother had tried her best to make me look good, I saw immediately that the other girls were more stylish and sophisticated, in their perky expensive outfits right out of the pages of *Seventeen* magazine. Some of them even wore dressy gloves and hats. Now I felt much less confident.

Nevertheless, I started the class very hopefully. I liked learning all the "tips" and being coached to fit in better. However, as the classes progressed, the things that the instructor said were essential to our success as girls seemed impossible to attain. We should walk and sit with the erectness of mannequins. We should keep our legs together at all times. We should always dress as if we were going out, even when we were just staying home. We should not wear eyeglasses unless absolutely necessary, and then take them off as soon as possible.

But how could I ride my bike in a skirt with my legs pressed together? If I got dressed up each day, my clothes would get ruined as I walked through the bakery. And eyeglasses—I was quite myopic and had finally convinced my parents I needed help. Now that I had glasses, I could see things at a distance. The first time I saw the individual leaves on a tree, I was overwhelmed with joy. Why did I have to go back to being in a blurry world?

The culmination of charm school was a big fashion show held in the store's auditorium, which had a proper runway and spotlights. The instructors would choose which students could be the models, dressed in the latest store fashions. Naturally, it was every girl's hope to be in the show. But at the end of the month, I was not one of the students chosen to perform. While part of me had never expected to be chosen over these obviously more poised and self-confident girls, nevertheless, I was crestfallen. Suddenly my mother's admonitions became increasingly strident and almost panicky.

"Linda, you've got to dress more feminine. Stop eating all that ice cream. You're going to get fat. And stop walking like a football player. No boys will ever be attracted to you like that. Why can't you be like the other girls?"

Although all the mothers I knew wanted their girls to look pretty and act properly, my mother seemed much more concerned. There were probably many factors behind this. She surely had unvoiced doubts about her own femininity—perhaps occasioned by a father who deserted her in the sensitive teenage years. She knew that her New York Jewishness felt out of place in Newark, giving her an assertive strength that my Italian female relatives did not possess to the same degree. But there may also have been something she recognized in me—a sensitive yet determined quality—which she feared would prevent me from leaping ahead culturally, making a "good marriage," and being more acceptable in American society.

Also, there was something else. I know she counted it a plus that, as a child, I took after my svelte Italian side, rather than the rounder Jewish side of her own family. Our physician, Dr. Schreck, continually warned that I was too thin, anemic, and run-down. He advised my parents to feed me eggnogs and steak to "build me up." But as puberty hit, I started to gain weight, and my mother had one more thing to worry about with me. Why did I have to pick *this* as the one way I would take after *her* side?

Her fear was contagious, and, for the first time, I began to think of particular foods as either "good" or "bad." I worked hard on my self-control, scrutinizing every meal and bite. I was determined not to end up as unhappy as the other overweight members of my family, for they seemed almost obsessed with what were actually only modest amounts of excess poundage. Although I did not go so far as the eating disorders of today's teenagers, the memories of my fear of getting heavy now make me realize that some nearly unattainable body standards have been around for a long time.

A year or so after my charm school debacle, my parents became really frustrated and decided to resort to "old country" ways. Without telling me, they conferred with some friends of theirs who had a twenty-year-old son studying to be a doctor. Ralph (I suppose his real name was Raphaello) had gone back to Italy to get his medical degree. But whenever he was in town visiting his parents, our two families were suddenly spending more time than usual together.

"Wouldn't it be nice, being married to a doctor?" my parents would ask each time Ralph was home. "You would have a beautiful house in the suburbs and not have to work."

Ralph seemed stuffy and formal to me, and his accent made me identify him with the older crowd of Italian immigrants in our neighborhood. Still, being with Ralph had its advantages, for when he was in town I was allowed to go out after dark unchaperoned. One night, sitting in his car,

I listened with great interest as Ralph told me that men in Italy always cooked on Sundays. This made me feel warmer toward him since my father, already in the food business, was often the cook in our family.

"Really?" I said. "That's very nice."

"Si . . ." he said in his heavy accent. "But . . . den . . . da women . . . dey heva to clin uppa da mess!" he said, laughing uproariously.

No more Ralph for me. Without explaining it to my parents, I refused to see him again. Yet I very much wanted to attract boys. So why did I continue to resist the feminine role as it was laid out for me by my parents, the church, and the neighborhood? I had no explanation. It just didn't feel right.

I did feel pretty when I dressed up, but it seemed so much trouble and so unnatural. Yet when I tried to adapt my circumstances to fit me better—letting my hair have its way, wearing pants and sneakers—I felt vaguely guilty, ugly, an embarrassment to my family. My natural inclinations added to the insecurities about my mixed-faith background to produce a kind of social stagnation. It did not help that my parents, in true immigrant fashion, largely kept me sheltered within the cloister of the family.

But I had to find a feminine image I could emulate so I could go into the world as a real woman, rather than a female impersonator. Increasingly, when I sat upstairs watching old movies on TV, I found myself drawn to actresses with strong, self-confident, and assertive images, like Katherine Hepburn. And on Sundays, as I sat in the little kitchen of the bakery, poring over *The New York Times Magazine*, I was impressed by the cool, sophisticated ladies I saw there. They wore simple, elegant outfits in neutral colors that were not too loud, not too gaudy, not too contrived. They even looked comfortable in an almost British, outdoorsy way. I felt sure I could be a woman like this, but there was no way my parents would let me spend the kind of money it would take to recreate their style.

I tried to simulate this sophisticated style with the cheaper department store offerings I could afford, using the few dollars my parents sometimes gave me for working in the bakery. It never came off quite right, and when I got home after an exhausting day trying to make it all work with sale clothes and knockoff bargain copies, inevitably my mother would disparage my choices, saying I looked "too plain."

"Why are you always covering up your looks? Why don't you wear some brighter colors? These clothes do nothing for you."

"Leave her alone, Gerry," my father would counter. "Let her do what she wants. She dresses fine. I like her as she is."

I am grateful now for my father's acceptance. Still, all along my parents tried everything they knew to improve my chances as a girl—not only charm school, but braces on my teeth, dance lessons, piano lessons, hand-me-downs from my stylish cousin. Ever hopeful, I would try my best for a while with each new plan. But in the end it was much more satisfying to go for a bike ride through Forest Hills in Newark—or posh Spring Lake at the shore—or get lost in a book, or watch an old movie on television. I could easily imagine that my true inner beauty was being discovered by Cary Grant, who would then surely ensconce me in a country mansion somewhere.

Smart Is Good

My parents believed the pharmacist was right about mixed marriages, and they told me I was smart. Perhaps it was this same pharmacist who told them about the private school in the nearby Forest Hills section. One spring day, my parents unexpectedly announced I would not be attending sixth grade at Summer Avenue Elementary School in the fall but would be advanced to seventh grade at Prospect Hill Country Day School. The "country day school" title was ironic, since the school was only about a half mile from Bloomfield Avenue.

But Prospect Hill had been in existence since the turn of the last century, when our neighborhood had been largely woods and fields. It was housed in what had once been the elegant home of the Clark family—of Coats and Clark Thread fame. Once enrolled, I spent much of my study-hall time in what had been their ballroom, trying to imagine their parties, their guests, their lifestyle.

My parents probably thought this was my only chance to merge with a "better crowd." It was certainly a better education, and it was also easier being a girl here. Beyond fourth grade, it was an all-girls' school, with no boys to impress. We wore navy blue wool blazers, a school crest proudly displayed on the pocket, with matching skirt, white button-down shirt, black-and-white saddle shoes, and tan raincoats. We were not allowed to wear makeup, and few girls bothered with "big" hair. Even better, the girls flaunted their intelligence, rather than hiding it. Some of them were Catholic and Italian-American, which was familiar.

But these were also the first rich girls I had ever met. They were from educated or at least privileged homes. Their parents were doctors, lawyers and, I now suspect, organized crime bosses. They arrived at school in taxis, while I walked over from the bakery. Their classy, refined manners impressed me. And on Fridays, when we weren't required to wear our uniforms, so did their clothes. Of course, I always hated Fridays, since I knew my clothes weren't up to theirs, but at least I only had to buy one special outfit, rather than a whole week's worth.

Our uniforms were supposed to provide a leveling effect, but it didn't work that way. My mother said the uniform skirt and jacket sold by the school was too expensive. She said I could easily buy the required articles at Orhbach's, the discount store downtown, and simply sew on the school crest. But the other girls could tell the difference, and they didn't mind mentioning it. It eventually dawned on me that my parents had asked for financial aid. For when I had the requisite yearly interview with the Headmistress, my mother would take me aside the night before, lower her voice, and say seriously: "Don't wear your best clothes tomorrow when you go to see her. Wear something old. I don't want her to think we're rich."

I felt conspicuous enough without this. Because I had skipped half of sixth grade in coming here, the intellectual challenges seemed almost insurmountable at first. My handwriting was below their standards. I was thrown into Latin and French classes without knowledge of English grammar. My math skills were inferior, and I took a class on Greek mythology without even knowing where Greece was on the map. I worked late every night to catch up. But my education advanced rapidly, and I reveled in all the new things I was learning. Here I was getting a serious education. In the Newark school, for all the teachers' heroic efforts, the thing I most remember is the lice infestation I picked up from some other kid. But there was also a negative toll, for I began to notice even more sharply the class, economic, and cultural differences that separated me from the other students. I started changing my pronunciation of words to fit in better. Sometimes it was hard to make the transition from school to home.

"Mom, I can't wait on customers right now. I have to do my math homework," I said one day, slipping into the soft, long *a* sound I used at school, instead of the flat, nasal *a* we used in my neighborhood. My mother thought I was "putting on airs."

"Maaaath" she said, caricaturing me. "Who do you think you are, anyway?"

An added problem was that most of the twelve girls in my private school class had been together since kindergarten. The only one to befriend me at the outset was another relative newcomer and the lone Jewish girl, Casey Herzfeld. She commuted from the Newark section known as Weequahic and once invited me to her home. It was my first time in that Jewish neighborhood. Their home was filled with music and books, had a real front porch, and yards, both back and front. We sat outdoors on a pretty wooden patio set and her mother served us tomato juice over ice in fine glassware, on a decorative tray, just as if we were real ladies.

Maybe Casey was the only Jewish girl in the class because of the strong Protestant heritage of this school. Many of the teachers had Anglo-Saxon surnames and reminded me of the bookish, stiff-upper-lip British women I saw in old movies on TV. Also, choir was compulsory, and the director made sure we learned many Reformation hymns. I had never heard them before and was strangely moved by the words. The hymns felt austere, serious, and somber but also seemed to go deep inside me and stir up some kind of a longing and courage. The school environment, combined with the improved education and inspiring hymns, made me equate— subliminally—intellect, culture, and Protestantism.

Because we were teen-aged girls with a burgeoning interest in boys, the school held frequent "mixers" with the private boys' schools in the area. They wanted to ensure that, right from the start, we would get used to the "right" kind of male. I dreaded these events. I couldn't see any benefit from it. What chance would a slightly pudgy, shy, squinting, frizzy-headed girl have at all these dances? Even if a boy did approach me, without my glasses on I wouldn't know it.

But at one Prospect Hill dance, with the boys and girls standing apart on opposite sides of the room, one brave, lone boy got up the nerve to venture across the ballroom floor. Unbelievably, he approached me, standing there with my classmates, and asked me to dance. I was so completely startled that without thinking I said "no" to his offer. Not only did my classmates think I was out of my mind, but the poor boy had to slink back across the floor, probably traumatized for life.

After three years at Prospect Hill, I realized I would never be fully accepted by these privileged girls. During school hours, things were okay. By adopting the posture of class clown, I had found a way to make friends. But aside from my visit to Casey—and one class sleepover in the undertaker's daughter's home (where our late-night forbidden treat was to go downstairs at midnight and view the bodies)—I was rarely invited to anyone's house. The fact that I was ashamed of our apartment over the bakery and rarely invited anyone to it added to my feelings of isolation.

The last straw came when an older student was suddenly called out of class one day. Rumor spread that her mother had gone down to the basement to get a box of tissues and found her father hanging dead. Some insisted it was a suicide, but others suggested darkly of involvement in organized crime. I had had enough of this place. Besides, I wanted a larger range of friends, and I wanted to be around boys on a more regular basis. I mentioned my discomfort about Prospect Hill to my parents. I had never admitted this before, and I could see they were surprised and disappointed. Yet I think Prospect Hill never suited my parents, either. Although they had attended the various events and fundraisers—bridge parties, fashion shows, formal banquets—it was evident that they were very nervous among the other parents.

Of course, they wouldn't consider sending me to Newark's Barringer High School, even though my father was a graduate and it was only a few blocks away, across the street from the cathedral. My parents had heard that drugs were being pushed in the rest rooms. But one day a Prospect Hill classmate, Susan Colatrello, said that next year, she was transferring to the public high school in Glen Ridge. It was a wealthy, residential enclave about ten miles away and they took commuters for a fee. Susan seemed very enthusiastic about it. The education was good, she said, they had sports teams and clubs, and best of all, it was coed. I presented this idea to my parents and, to my surprise, they agreed.

No Country Club

I started tenth grade at Glen Ridge High School. To get there I rode the public bus straight north on Bloomfield Avenue, passing through the northern section of Newark, then Bloomfield, and Montclair. Just like in the opening credits montage for HBO's *The Sopranos*, the businesses and houses became progressively larger, farther apart, and more affluent-looking the farther I went along my journey. I had the sense that I was moving up, even if it was only a temporary respite from Newark.

The school lived up to its good reputation. The teachers were stimulating, and we had team sports, social groups, and clubs. I was happy to go to school with boys again, although it was a little intimidating to meet girls who actually wore, on a daily basis, the expensive clothes I saw advertised in *The New York Times*. Glen Ridge gave me an even broader look at the world of the privileged. No one knew that many years later this same town would become infamous, its good reputation tarnished when members of the football team raped a handicapped girl. Was I surprised? It's hard to say. Had I seen behavior among its elite, privileged young people that might escalate, without the proper adult supervision, into such an atrocity? Possibly.

At the time, Glen Ridge was a shock to me, for I had been very sheltered within my family and ethnic neighborhood. This high school was where I first encountered WASPs, as the dominant group and learned where I stood in the wider, American social hierarchy. My orientation started on the very first day.

"Hmmm, *Mercadante*," said one of the popular girls at lunch. "What kind of name is that?"

"Italian," I said confidently.

"I bet you're Catholic. You're not from this town, are you? Where do you live?" she continued with raised eyebrows.

"I come up on the bus from Newark," I answered, with less enthusiasm.

"Oh, well, it's good you don't live here. We don't have many Catholics in our town. The most important church in Glen Ridge is Congregational. And you couldn't become a member in our country club. It doesn't take Italians *or* Catholics," she said smiling smugly.

"We don't take Jews either," said another girl sitting nearby.

After that, I kept a rather low profile. I never mentioned that the other half of my family was Jewish. Of course I was, and am now still, ashamed that I hid my heritage, but I was faced with a dilemma. I already had one strike against me for being Italian. Strike two was being from Newark. I could not afford to reveal the third strike of being Jewish as well. As a teenager finally hoping to be "normal"—which meant fitting into the wider American social scene—I expected

Glen Ridge to provide me with the required breakthrough. While the education I received and the wider range of activities were helpful, my hoped-for social breakthrough did not happen. Although I joined every girls' sports teams, won a letter, enthusiastically attended football games, performed in a school dance, and got good grades, the only classmates I saw after school were the two other girls who also commuted by bus from Newark. Likewise, although I was on friendly terms with many of the boys while at school, not one of them asked me out.

To be honest, I did have *one* date in high school. It was for the Junior Prom, arranged by a sympathetic English teacher, Mr. Tarrant, with his friend's son who visiting from out of town. But the boy's parents were afraid to let him drive to Newark to pick me up, and even my teacher was reluctant to enter the city at night. So instead, my parents drove me to Mr. Tarrant's house, where we reconnoitered for the prom. Being from Newark was starting to look like the strike against me that was worse than being either Italian-Catholic or Jewish.

Part of it was probably because things were changing fast in Newark. We did not know that the 1967 Newark riots were just on the horizon. Even prior to that, however, the city's residents had been moving away in droves, and our neighborhood was visibly declining. At first, the full implications of Newark's "white flight" were not obvious. Because public transportation was good and distances between towns were short, people could move to nearby suburbs and still continue to commute downtown. We could not predict that soon the suburbs would no longer need the city for work or shopping, and only those unable to leave would be left to witness the increasing urban blight.

As our North Ward neighborhood continued to decline and my parents got older, I became afraid their shop would be robbed or they would become crime victims. I begged them to consider relocating their business, but they would not consider it. They figured that no suburban neighborhood—which they presumed was filled with WASPs—would provide enough business to sustain an Italian pastry shop. But even our ethnic neighborhood was not supporting the bakery as it once had. We had been getting less and less walk-in trade, formerly the mainstay of all the shops on Bloomfield Avenue. In addition, customers who once had lived in the neighborhood, then moved away, still wanted to enjoy our pastries but were no longer willing to drive into Newark to our store. They made increasing demands to have everything delivered. My mother, who had formerly been happy to fill phone orders to be picked up by these customers, was getting exasperated.

"No, we *can't* afford to deliver just a few pastries," I heard her say one day. "You *can* drive down here. It's safe. You can park right out front," she said. She paused, probably listening to the caller's worries, and then ended the conversation by shouting into the mouthpiece: "Listen . . . What do you think we are, chopped liver? We *live* here!"

Chapter Four

Flying Out of Newark

Going to college provided the perfect excuse for getting away from Newark. My parents didn't want me to go far, but they were willing to let me live on the campus of some nearby school. Their first choice for me was Douglas College in New Brunswick, about an hour away from Newark. Since Rutgers, the state university, still only admitted males, this was its female branch. Although Princeton—a school I would later attend for doctoral work—was also nearby, it was not even in my frame of reference. I never dreamed I could attend an Ivy League school, and, besides, it was still all-male as well. Instead, I followed the advice of a guidance counselor and looked at state universities and small colleges in surrounding states.

My parents and I enjoyed visiting colleges. I got the sense from them that I was about to do something very important. When we explored the various campuses, my father was concerned that everything be safe and comfortable. But my mother seemed excited, imagining what a fun life a student could have. She had always wanted me to have more friends and never understood why the school friends I spoke about never came over in the evenings, or on weekends and vacations.

"When I was your age," she would say, "my friends and I would walk arm-in-arm over the bridge into Manhattan, go to the movies, and then to the Automat for a snack. I spent lots of time in their apartments, and sometimes they visited mine. Why don't you do things like this?"

I couldn't explain my feelings to her, but I had the same hope for me as she did. Maybe my social life would finally begin, now that there would be no Newark or bakery grime to haunt me. Yet even with my minimalist social life, my parents were proud of me and especially my academic achievements. They were proud of themselves, too, for producing a "college girl." Nobody in our family's older generation had anything beyond high school. A few times my father had hinted that he once wanted to be a doctor. Yet neither of my parents had actually expected to earn college degrees. They were realistic about the prospects they had growing up. Under the circumstances, both my parents were gratified they had graduated from high school, especially my father, who had to earn his diploma at night and in a new language. They were also proud they had carved out a successful business.

I don't remember feeling ashamed that my parents did not have college degrees, and, even though I complained about it, I was proud of their business, too. But many of the students I had met at Prospect Hill and Glen Ridge had parents or at least fathers with college degrees and active professional lives. I sensed that these parents were more aware of the options and opportunities available for their children and could help them. I realize now, as I didn't then, that I was at a disadvantage, doing something for which my parents could offer me no guidance. Instead, like most first-generation children, I had to forge a path through uncharted territory—trying to negotiate between my parents' narrower expectations and society's broader opportunities. At the time, however, I just felt lucky that they wanted me to go to college and were willing to pay for it.

My aunts and uncles, along with my parents, had spent countless hours over the dinner table convincing each other that in the modern world a Bachelor's degree was the key to success. Of course, most of them also thought that, for girls, the main purpose of college was to find a "nice college boy" and earn the "Mrs." degree. Still, they said, it wouldn't hurt for us girls to get some job training "just in case." Both sides of my family were practical, but they saw education as an important route to full assimilation. According to the statistics of that period, Jews routinely favored higher education for their children, no matter what their background or financial condition. However, this expectation was not so common for Italian Americans. Many of this ethnic group felt it was more important to keep their children close to home, especially the girls. This caused a dilemma for intelligent or ambitious girls. They often had to deal not only with a lack of emotional and financial support from the family, but also their own guilt for going against parental wishes.

Fortunately, my father's family deviated from the Italian-American norm with regard to higher education, but they held fiercely to the Italian-American norm that fully expected all their children to stay close to home—not just during college but afterward as well. Moving out of Newark was okay— in fact upward mobility practically demanded it—but my parents expected I would return to New Jersey immediately upon graduation and stay within an hour of them forever. One other thing was completely clear to all the relatives: none of them wanted their children to work as hard as they had to. "A nice clean job"—that's what they wanted for us, and college was the key. I agreed completely. I liked school and was good at it. And I certainly didn't want to work in a bakery all my life. But what would I do if I didn't find someone to marry immediately? My parents were clear that I would work until the right guy came along. My mother had

worked before marriage and talked with a sense of importance about the jobs she had held—secretary, telephone op-
erator, and factory worker. This period had clearly been the
highlight of her life, even though she had lived at home and
contributed much of her income to her mother's and sister's
support. She described a glamorous life as a single woman,
with nice clothes, restaurant meals, and frequent outings with
friends. She wanted that for me—and more.

With a college degree, I was expected to move a step beyond my parents. However, according to them, there were
only two acceptable professional jobs for a girl, teaching
or nursing. We didn't know any Italian or Jewish nurses,
and all the relatives agreed the work was too hard, still in
the hands-on category that they wanted us to escape. But
teaching . . . now, that was different. It was "a good job for a
girl." A teacher worked with books and little children. She
had her summers off. When she got married, she could quit,
yet she'd still have "something to fall back on if, God forbid,
she needed it."

All of us girl cousins were planning to become teachers. I never even thought about doing something else. But
I rebelled when it came to choosing a school in New Jersey.
Although there were many colleges offering teaching degrees nearby, I chose American University in Washington,
D.C. My parents adjusted surprisingly well, reasoning that
Washington still was on the East Coast corridor, only about
four hours away, so they could easily drive me there, plus
there was good train and airline service between the cities,
should I want to come home for the weekends. To celebrate
my admission they bought me an entire set of hard, blue
plastic American Tourister luggage, which gave my move
their stamp of approval.

When school started in September, it was exhilarating
yet a bit frightening once my parents moved me into the

dorm and left. For the first few months, I did travel home frequently. But once I settled in and made friends, a new world opened up for me. I began to meet interesting people who, though they also adhered to clear gender differences, seemed to allow a bit more latitude. It was the late 1960s, and the girls at college were more like what I wanted to be. They wore pants, loafers, and bulky sweaters. They played tennis and took long walks. They felt free to let their brains show, and they expected me to show mine. Also, they didn't complain if I wore my eyeglasses all the time.

My best friend and roommate, Judy, was Jewish, as were most of my other friends. I realized I was often drawn to Jewish people, but I didn't know what to make of it. We went to restaurants and movies together, got involved in protests and politics, discussed deep issues. Best of all, my life with boys finally began. Removed from the stigma of Newark and the bakery, I was just another girl in the dorm.

Girls in White Hoods

Before I left for college, my mother had given me one stern warning: she told me not to join a sorority. "They're all anti-Semitic," she said. "They won't let you join if they know you are Jewish."

I figured she couldn't possibly be right. After all, she had never been to college. At my school, social life revolved around the Greek groups, and I was desperate to make up for lost time. I went out for "Rush" and tried all five of the sororities. I was surprised when I got accepted into one of the larger ones, known as a "Christian" sorority. It hadn't seemed unusual to me that there were Christian ones and Jewish ones. I don't remember discussing religion with anyone, but they must have checked each girl's record before making their selections. For my part, I was surprised that the

Jewish ones rejected me. But I was just happy to be accepted into a popular group. Suddenly I had lots of dates from boys in our brother fraternities, which were the "Christian" ones. There appeared to be no cross-dating between the Jewish and Christian Greek groups.

The pledging phase, which lasted much of the first year, was fun, and the hazing was minimal. After many months, we were ready for the secret initiation. We "pledges" were blindfolded and driven to somewhere out in the suburbs. Still blindfolded, we were led down some stairs to a dark basement. Without being able to see anything, we stood in a circle while many people silently filed in. When the blindfolds were removed, we were surrounded by young women dressed in floor-length white robes with hoods hiding their faces, similar to those worn by the Ku Klux Klan.

After some opening remarks, one young woman came forward and began to read the bylaws out of a large, impressive book. The laws stated emphatically that this group was only for white women of Christian heritage. She indicated that others were explicitly excluded. While I had noticed that the sororities seemed segregated, I didn't know there were actual rules governing this. As I stood there in the circle, a deep wave of fear passed through me.

The aura caused by the hidden drive, the blindfolding, the white-hooded people, the gravity of their attitude, and the stern-sounding bylaws, intimidated me. What if they found out? What would happen to me? I realized with shock that my mother had been right. But I was too scared, and it was too late, for me to do anything about it. If I were blackballed at this stage, I would have no social life at all for the whole four years of college. I couldn't afford to repeat my high school experience. So, feeling sick and alone, I accepted my pin. So did another of my fellow pledges who later that spring tried to bring her African-American boyfriend to the Greek ball.

When she was censured and then made to resign, I saw the results of rebellion.

Once again I had been frightened off from revealing my Jewish heritage. Although I had legitimately and sincerely converted and was, by then, secure in my Catholic identity, I still felt twinges of guilt. In the end, the exclusivism of the Greek groups turned me off, and, little by little, I withdrew from activities—except for formal occasions and mixers where boys might be involved. Instead, I stuck with my Jewish friends who did not belong to any particular group. In the end, my girlfriends were Jewish, and my boyfriends were Christian. I noticed this about myself but didn't think much about it. Being split down the middle was just me.

It takes an exceptional young person to be completely self-revealing, especially in a high school or college atmosphere. The price seems too high, and it is easier to just fit in. But I wonder what would have happened had I been more honest or at least shared my misgivings about the initiation ceremony. Little did I know that other pledges had been equally disconcerted by the same thing. During the writing of this book, I received an email from a sorority sister. Although we had completely lost touch, she was getting together a group to have an informal reunion. I knew it would take me considerable effort to attend, but I thought it would present an incomparable opportunity to revisit that period. Most of these women still lived on the East Coast, so the reunion was held in a large hotel far out on Long Island. I drove all the way from Ohio in hurricane conditions so I would not miss this event.

The group was not large, and we spent nearly every waking hour of a long weekend together. Each one of us got a chance to tell her entire life story since graduation. The expected tales of marriages, children, careers, and divorces were shared. Given my low profile in college, the women were amazed that I had earned a Ph.D., become ordained, and now was teaching in a Protestant seminary. But the biggest surprise came when we began to reminisce about our sorority experience. To a person, each of us admitted she had been shocked, frightened, and completely dismayed by the rituals, outfits, and bylaws of our initiation event. We were amazed that we had had such similar reactions, yet not one of us had felt confident or brave enough to share this with her other sisters. Was it because we then lived in an age of more conformity, when fitting in was more important than standing out? Was it because we were the kind of young women who needed the acceptance and shelter of a Greek group? Or was it because the sorority system itself impressed upon us the dangers of nonconformity and rebellion? All of us remembered vividly the one young woman who had brought an African American to the dance and was made to resign.

Yet for all our conformity and lack of self-revealing, we had gone on from this repressive place to break stereotypes, find careers, leave problematic marriages, and learn ways to support ourselves and even thrive. I can credit the women's movement for some of this, giving us the courage and example to break out of our societal molds. But I also realized that I shouldn't be too quick to judge the young women who—even now after years of our efforts to secure women's freedom—can often seem conformist, unformed, or acquiescent to society's demands on them. We can't know the end from the beginning, and it can still take a long time today for young women to grow into their potential.

Education Major

My parents had insisted I enroll for a teaching degree, and I did. But I soon found the elementary education courses not to my liking. In order to free up time to take subjects in which I was more interested, I tested out of my humanities requirements and suddenly had lots of space for electives. My vocational future started to look promising when one day, after the final exam in my huge "Introduction to Psychology" course, the professor called me in. I was impressed that she was a woman, and elated when she said, "You got the highest grade in this class. You have a real talent for psychology. Why don't you switch your major?"

I called my parents and excitedly relayed the professor's advice. They listened briefly and said, "That's nice, Linda, but it's not a good idea. You need a Ph.D. to do anything in that field."

That answered that. I was disappointed but acquiescent. They were paying, after all. I just still felt lucky to be in college and pleased that I would be qualified for a job afterwards. Maybe I would meet an interesting guy who had an important job and could take me to exciting places. Teaching would be fine, I thought. And I couldn't imagine what else I would be allowed to do. No one but that female psychology professor had ever told me differently.

One day, after I received an "A" on a paper on James Joyce's *Ulysses*, the professor of advanced English stopped me on my way out of the room.

"Good job," he said. "By the way, what is your major?"

When I told him it was elementary education, he looked disgusted and said, "If I had known that, I wouldn't have given you an 'A.'"

In my senior year, my academic advisor suggested I try to qualify for teaching certificates in several states, because "you don't know where your husband will want to live." I had never mentioned any marital plans to him. Although I was growing increasingly uncomfortable with the path my parents had laid out for me, I still tried outwardly to conform. It was like living a dual life, as I prepared for a teaching career, while also making forays into areas that interested me more. It did not occur to me—yet—to try a completely different path, because, to be honest, there did not seem to be many. I had never met a professional woman, and newspapers still advertised jobs in columns marked "Male" and "Female."

Perhaps I did not focus on my career options because I felt driven to catch up socially. I had barely dated before college and had never had a real "relationship" with a boy. While I had many males in my life, they were mostly all relatives. Outside of that, I was clueless. So I entered the college dating world enthusiastically. I had lost all my baby fat and was working on my appearance. Recently, my parents had opened up a second store in our building. Since it sold women's clothing, suddenly I was able to be consistently well dressed, which gave me more confidence.

My first year I promptly fell in love with a Protestant boy. From New England, wealthy, with his own sailboat, he captivated me. Apparently, I captivated him, too, and we decided to marry right after we graduated. But Richard's mother, who was a divorced single parent, insisted her son end the relationship. Since I was a Catholic, she told him, I would never be allowed to divorce him if things didn't work out. Unfortunately, in a cruel irony of fate that seemed almost a mockery of his mother's worry, things *didn't* work out for the two of us, because, as Richard was driving his little sports car home to visit his mother and confront the matter, he hit a truck and was killed instantly.

After that devastation, I stuck a little closer to home, figuring I'd have better luck if I dated only Catholics. I don't remember if I thought then that this tragedy had a deeper meaning, but I felt sure I had stepped out of my appropriate social bounds. After a few false starts, in my third year I fell in love with Sandy, a devout Catholic attending nearby

Georgetown University. His father was a career diplomat and stationed in the U.S. embassy in Paris. Sandy planned to follow the same career path. He introduced me to European culture, food, and new ideas. We planned to marry as soon as I graduated. I was a year ahead of him and was willing to support him by teaching as he prepared for the Foreign Service. Although our families were worlds apart in just about every way, Sandy never suggested my background was a problem. I adored him. It was especially wonderful that he was comfortable visiting me on school vacations in our apartment in Newark, although I'm sure it was quite strange to him. When his parents sailed for Europe after a lengthy furlough in the U.S., we saw them off. As the horn blew and we prepared to disembark, they took us aside and warned us not to do anything drastic while they were gone. During Christmas vacation of my senior year, Sandy went to visit his parents in Paris and from there sent back a letter ending the relationship. He gave no reason, and I never understood why. I took it extremely hard, and the pain lingered for years.

These two events had a profound effect on my faith. I entered college a practicing Catholic and regularly attended the "folk mass" in our school chapel. It seemed modern and I liked the doughnuts afterward. But one morning shortly after Sandy had ended our relationship, I was at mass reciting the Hail Mary when I had a startling insight. If Mary was the church's epitome of womanhood, my chances were hopeless. There was no way I could become the mother of God, nor did I want to be a perpetual virgin. And what about my two broken engagements? Where had God been in that? I made an appointment to speak with the priest about this. To my dismay, he didn't have much to offer, except to assure me that all of it was God's will. But if these heartbreaks were God's will, God couldn't care about me very much. How could God have let me lose the only two boys that had ever loved me? Here I was, about to graduate, and half my life plan was in ruins. After that, I didn't think too much about God, didn't go to church, and gradually stopped focusing on religion at all.

I felt like a failure, but there was nothing else to do but carry on with the rest of the plan. Dutifully, I applied to teach fourth grade in the excellent Chevy Chase school system. It seemed enough that at least I would not have to return to Newark. And a teaching job would fulfill some of my parents' expectations. I interviewed and was offered the job, but with the unsigned contract still on my desk, I began to have second thoughts. Teaching was supposed to be what I did to "help my husband" until I had children. But I would have no husband now, at least for the foreseeable future. My parent-approved life trajectory had fizzled and, out of desperation, I was feeling a bit reckless. So when I noticed that job recruiters were coming to my campus, I checked out their listings. Although I noted on the sign-up sheet that mostly boys were taking these interviews, I figured it couldn't hurt for me to put my name down.

Great Stewardess

One of the recruiters on campus was United Airlines, so I signed up for an interview. An airline sounded exciting, but I had no real plan of how to present myself—an elementary education major, with a second major in English. This didn't seem to qualify me. I had only been on an airplane a couple of times, and that was all I knew. When the day came, I was the only girl waiting with all the boys in the long hall outside the interviewing offices. Eventually, my name was called. I got up and entered the room, taking a seat near a small desk. Behind it sat a handsome man dressed in an expensive suit. He seemed mildly surprised to see me but asked obligingly what I would like to do for United Airlines. Feeling at a loss and very nervous, I reached for something that sounded important.

"Oh well . . . I would like to be . . . uh . . . in management," I said. That sounded good. I felt pleased with my spontaneous answer.

Without missing a beat, the man smiled down at me and said smoothly, "Oh, we don't take girls in management. But you'd make a great airline stewardess."

This idea did not appeal to me at all. I had seen what stewardesses did: they served food on airplanes. On the contrary, I was envisioning an important position in an office and perhaps some business travel. I never voiced any of this, but with a touch of desperation, I countered, "But I have a college degree."

"Oh, most of our girls do," he said, reassuringly.

That was it. The only objection I could think of was shot down. More significantly, it began to dawn on me that here was someone important, someone from the wider world of mainstream America, who thought I was feminine enough. This attractive man must be seeing something in me that I didn't know was there. Suddenly, I got an image of myself walking confidently down an airplane aisle, dressed in a smart suit, looking poised and beautiful. The picture was surprisingly compelling, and it lured me in. Most important, it was a way out of my dilemma, for here was something else I could do besides teaching and something, I was sure, that would not require me to go back to Newark. I asked a few questions, thought about it briefly, and then signed up on the spot.

I told myself that my parents wouldn't care all that much. I even thought they might be pleasantly surprised that I had passed such an important femininity test. Wrong. Not only did they feel that all their money had been wasted, but they said only loose women went into such a line of work. Oh. I had never heard that. But it was too late. My imagination was already in the air. I could admit to myself, finally, that I felt too young to be stuck in a classroom all day. I would never meet any men my age in an elementary school.

So, over my parents' disgust and anger, that summer I went to the United Airlines stewardess school in Des Plaines, Illinois. A month later, after "stew school" graduation— which my parents, on principle, refused to attend in spite of the free ticket United offered them—we were allowed to bid for our home base. Many glamorous bases were available to me, such as Los Angeles, as well as such urban centers as Chicago. But—in a bit of unconscious repentance—I bid for Newark and, not surprisingly, got it.

I tried to get an apartment in Manhattan, to take full advantage of my new exciting life, but prices were far beyond the means of a beginning flight attendant. So, with a classmate from stewardess school, I took a furnished apartment in a run-down neighborhood of Irvington, an older city with a reputation just a tiny bit better than Newark's. We tried to ignore our surroundings but instead, with great expectations, settled in to enjoy the exciting career they had promised us. My good fortune seemed endless. Instead of having to stay in Newark and the bakery, or be hidden away in a classroom, I would now be able to travel the world, meet interesting people, and maybe marry one of them. I found it gratifying to have independence, to be earning a salary, and to be noticed by everyone when I was in uniform. Suddenly I didn't mind so much being seen primarily as an attractive young woman.

I now think it was fortunate that I took such a stereotypical female job as my first. The admiring glances from men, the smart uniforms, and the fact that being a stewardess, at the time, was considered the epitome of femininity was good for me. It erased any lingering doubts about my being acceptably female. No longer was I an ambivalent half-and-half misfit but a poised and attractive young woman with considerable independence. Although the job turned out to be wretched in many ways, it had this important side benefit: it served me in my female identity the way military training or the football team serves many males who feel inadequate to meet society's gender standards.

In retrospect, I shouldn't have been surprised that the job was not as romantic and fulfilling as I had anticipated. They drilled into us at stew school that, to keep this job, we had to stay at the weight they specified, wear only contact lenses and never eyeglasses, don full makeup including false eyelashes and bright lipstick, wear girdles and heels, not get angry, and smile no matter what. If we married, got to age thirty-five, or became pregnant, it was over.

For a while, it seemed a small price to pay for the privilege of travel and adventure, something I felt I could never achieve on my own. But it gradually dawned on me how exhausting, unpredictable, and often demeaning this job really was. Many passengers treated us like servants, expecting instant attention or special privileges. Others saw us primarily as sex symbols. Some women seemed to resent us. A few times, I saw a man watching us with a little mirror aimed up our skirts as we moved down aisles. Some male passengers would squeeze past us more closely than was necessary. Other passengers were polite and respectful, but few expected us to be more than pretty faces who were quick with their food.

Layovers were particularly difficult, since we found ourselves with much time on our hands in motels far from city centers. Sometimes, strange men came to our doors or found out our room numbers and called, demanding we come out and drink with them.

"Come on, stew, I know you're in there," demanded one at the cheap motel we were sent to for our layover in the Akron-Canton area. He repeatedly banged on the door until we called the front desk.

Laughing, the attendant said, "Well, if you *really* don't want to see him, I'll send someone up to make him leave."

Hotels did not yet have vans, so all our ground transportation was done by cabs. But although many cab drivers were polite and helpful, they could also be a problem. Often there were several of us crowded into a small vehicle, two in front alongside the driver and three in back.

"Oh, I'll bet your feet are tired after all that walking in heels," one cabby said to my partner sitting in the middle on the front bench seat. "Here, let me rub them for you."

He reached down and pulled her foot up onto his lap while we all sat there scared and shocked, waiting for our chance to get out, but not really protesting. After all, we had been admonished in our training to present a benign, pleasing appearance to the public, or risk censure and even dismissal.

Besides the harassment, we were often stranded at odd hours in unfamiliar places because of weather or mechanical problems. We learned to nap sitting up in terminal waiting rooms, using our hard plastic purses as pillows, go without food for long hours—crew meals were sometimes provided for pilots but not for flight attendants—and work way beyond the point of fatigue. It became a burden to keep up the façade of being a combination geisha, cheerleader, and waitress, ever accessible and pleasant to everyone, no matter how tired or hassled, but just out of reach.

Although many pilots were thoughtful and benign, there

were some who did not make things any easier. On my first day, right before the gate agents allowed the passengers to board, one of them decided to subject me to his little initiation ritual for new stewardesses. He suddenly came out of the cockpit, lifted me up, and threw me into one of the large, open overhead bins. Dressed in the short, red one-piece dress with big white stripe down the middle that passed for a uniform, I was still struggling to get down just as the passengers began boarding. Later that day another pilot backed me into the "blue room"—jargon for the tiny lavatory—and closed the door on the two of us. Pelvis to pelvis, he made it clear who was in charge.

On board, most pilots expected prompt meal service and deference. In the hotel, some pilots simply wanted to rest, but others wanted a party-girl drinking partner, or more. I successfully avoided these extra-curricular demands, but it made for lonely layovers. Often I'd find myself visiting museums or bookstores during my free time, and doing a lot of reading. It was hard to have an ongoing social life at home, too, since we were away so much. However, like the rest of the flight attendants, I loved the travel. Besides layovers all over the U.S., I took many trips, at bargain rates, with other stewardesses to Europe, Asia, and Latin America. So, while the job was disappointing, I didn't know what else I could do. I liked my new freedom and the benefits too much. Amazingly, I still wasn't connecting the gender dots.

Chapter Five

Spiritually Seeking

I met George in a bar. It was early in my airline career, when I was just twenty-one. I was spending a weekend at the beach, as I often did, staying at my aunt's house in Belmar. George was at the bar alone, but he and my date had gotten into a game of darts, the object being that the winner bought me a drink. By the end of the evening, I learned that George's father had owned a very small amusement park across the street from the beach. During our summers at the shore, my parents had brought us there nearly every day. I clearly remember being in awe of the boy several years older than me who drove the kiddy train, my favorite ride. George insisted that he had been that boy.

This coincidence prompted me to give George my phone number. Although he was only twenty-nine, he seemed awfully mature to me. What added to this impression was that George was a recent widower with a toddler daughter. His wife, who had a chronic illness, had died in bed while he was out bowling, a terrible fact he did not discover until he awoke the next morning. Unfortunately, in his grief he had begun drinking too much. I felt terribly sorry for him, but also felt this was someone I could trust, someone older, wiser, and knowledgeable about life and death.

George was impressed that I was a flight attendant. Soon we began dating, and it pleased me that I seemed to make him happy. But he was only a high school graduate and had gone to work immediately without even considering college. His mother commented that her son was always attracted to women who were smarter than he was. Although George wasn't exactly the type of man I was hoping to meet, I did find him familiar and comfortable.

It helped that he came from the Jersey shore, a place I associated with relaxation and pleasure. Our tastes in food and furnishings were compatible. We rarely argued, and George was generous and warm. He often surprised me with stylish clothes that fit perfectly. But underneath it all, I think the reason I kept dating him was because I felt safe. I knew he wouldn't abandon me as Sandy had done. With my encouragement, George stopped drinking and enrolled at a nearby college, Montclair State.

After several months of dating, however, I became increasingly nervous and frustrated. It was partly because I wanted more in a relationship but also because I could see his family was looking at me as a potential stepmother. Having met George's mother, sister, and daughter, I could see they were expecting this to be more than simply a short-term dating relationship. I wasn't able to see myself in that arrangement. So, to get away from both George and New Jersey, I put in for a transfer to San Francisco. Although it was a prime base, my request was granted, and soon I was flying out there to look for an apartment. I found one in a great neighborhood with two other flight attendants. We had views of San Francisco Bay and were within walking distance of trendy shops and restaurants. I was ecstatic that I had escaped my destiny. No bakery, no Newark, no Italian guy from New Jersey. Finally the glamorous life I had dreamed of would begin.

George, of course, was not happy about this. But he offered to drive my Firebird out there for me, and, against my better judgment, I accepted. He drove straight through, leaving his toddler daughter with his mother. Once there, George set about his campaign, taking me out to fancy restaurants, taking trips around the Bay area, and generally making himself an essential presence in my life. When my mother called one day and pointedly asked if George were there, he grabbed the phone and said:

"Oh, don't worry, Mrs. Mercadante, we're going to get married. Everything is okay."

After he hung up, he held me down on the bed and kept repeating "Say yes, say yes," until I did. The scary part was that it seemed inevitable. I was simply fulfilling the mandate I had been given since I was a child. So, dutifully, I put in for a transfer back to Newark and quickly got it. I fell into confused despair as we drove back across the Bay, heading east to New Jersey. I had tried to run away, but I had been caught. I had tried to rebel, but obviously I couldn't pull it off for very long. Still, I was supposed to be happy. This was what I had been raised for.

There was no doubt in anyone's mind that we would have a big Italian wedding, just as my cousins had. But even while the preparations were under way, I wasn't sure I was doing the right thing. I asked everyone for opinions. One kindly pilot took me out to dinner and said, "He just wants someone to take care of his child. Don't you realize that?" My cousins, on the other hand, approved, saying it would be hard to find someone more suitable than George. My parents declined to offer an opinion. But it wasn't until my best friend, Judy, said, "Well, if it doesn't work out, you could always get a divorce," that I figured I could take a chance and go ahead with it.

On the day of the wedding, someone gave me a Valium—something I had never taken—to calm me down, so I could walk down the aisle of Sacred Heart Cathedral. I felt beautiful, and George looked so happy. Everyone else seemed to be happy, too. So I disregarded my feelings as foolish and figured I must be doing the right thing. At the reception, held in a banquet hall I had always dreamed about, we had our first dance to the then-popular tune "Leaving on a Jet Plane," a song George insisted upon. I hated it, for I knew I had tried to leave on a jet plane—but hadn't gotten far. During the dance, George's little daughter ran out onto the floor, trying to separate us. Although her grandmother laughed and pulled her away, I felt icy cold inside, afraid, trapped in a nightmare from which I hoped I would wake up soon. But I didn't. Even now, I still marvel at the power of expectation, circumstance, and the training to ignore one's feelings that prevented me from acting on my gut knowledge that I was doing the wrong thing.

Life moved on in the expected pattern. We rented an apartment in Parsippany, within reach of Newark Airport for me and Montclair State for George. He took a job with the college maintenance department and pursued a business degree. As for his daughter, his mother graciously offered to keep her for our first year of marriage so we could get settled. On weekends, she would visit, and although she was sweet and easygoing, the whole thought of being an adoptive mother scared me to the bone. Everyone else, however, seemed to be happy.

Sisterhood Is Powerful

I cooked big Italian meals, entertained relatives, shopped for furniture, and kept working for the airline. I was pretty much doing what I had been trained to do, and it wasn't hard. Although I realized the life-plan I had been given didn't feel as satisfying as I had been led to believe, I figured the fault was mine. After all, my cousins and friends seemed happy with their lives.

But a book changed everything. One day on a layover, I was browsing in a progressive bookstore and happened upon a copy of *Sisterhood Is Powerful* by Robin Morgan. The title touched me in a way I couldn't explain, so I bought it. As I read the essays, my world changed. The tone was vehement and forceful. It covered every aspect of life, from the church to the bedroom, showing how repressive gender roles constricted and deformed females.

As I read, I began to see myself and my situation in an entirely different light. I had never heard the word "sexism" before, but now I could see that much of my lifelong frustration, second-class treatment, sense of inadequacy as a female, and feelings of being trapped, stemmed from this previously unnamed societal force.

It wasn't just my work and my lifestyle that were wrong, it was also my whole framework of meaning. For according to this book, all religion, including the Catholic Church, was clearly part of the problem. Suddenly, my lax attendance at mass was given a whole new justification. Although it's not unusual for a twenty-something young person to put religion aside, preoccupied as they are with mating and career, now the whole issue was re-opened, and it didn't look very good. I didn't renounce my faith, but I began to question the church, which had once been my anchor. I questioned the values I had been given, the focus on family, the expectation that I would produce children, dress well, live in the suburbs, and be happy enough.

Learning about feminism was depressing and liberating at the same time. The veil in front of my eyes had been ripped away. Now the gender dots *did* connect. Sort of like the Baltimore Catechism, this new ideology gave me a way to see the whole picture. It made sense of my world in a way that fit the reality I had always known but never understood.

Suddenly it became intolerable to go to work every day, in the little dress with the ridiculous white plastic cap, heels that made all the standing and walking uncomfortable, and people who thought we were nothing but vacuous space cadets with good bodies. As with many converts, I could not stop talking and thinking about my discovery. I evaluated everything in light of this new version of reality. One Saturday afternoon, I attended the bridal shower of a friend. It felt like the millionth such event, because everyone I knew was getting married. As we sat at my friend's feet, watching her open gift after gift of domestic accoutrements for her coming life in the suburbs, I felt like a tribal attendant, offering up the vestal virgin on an altar of toaster ovens and blenders.

My conversion led me into an entirely new world for women. Those of us with raised consciousnesses were serious about the work ahead, yet giddy with expectation. We didn't know what the coming world would look like, but we had an idea how it would feel. We could finally live as free and full people, with equal opportunity, no longer judged by our appearance, comfortable and happy in our own female bodies. Women bonded with other women, with much less regard than before for religious, ethnic, or social backgrounds. The only important separation was the separation between us and the women who did not yet "get it." Many of the women who didn't get it were my co-workers on the airline. I had to get out of this world.

George agreed, but for totally different reasons. Although he had enjoyed telling his friends he was marrying a stewardess, he had found my unpredictable schedule and layovers in other cities troublesome. However, my new feminist ideology upset him much more. I was growing increasingly touchy about gender roles, which I had previously taken for granted. I did not despise marriage but was disgusted with the attenuated lives my married women friends and relatives seemed to be living.

George approved of my plan to quit the airline. If I had a ground job, he reasoned, I would calm down. Still, I wasn't sure what I could do instead. I had already decided I didn't want to teach, but I wasn't trained for anything else. All I knew was I didn't want to be an airline stewardess anymore. After three years, I was tired of being treated like a servant and tired of the erratic schedule. I was tired of the supervisor checking my weight and even my underwear, tired of having to wear false eyelashes, contact lenses, and lipstick all the time.

But the extensive travel and independence of the job had given me confidence. Visiting cities all over America had exposed me to new trends. And I had found I was good at engaging complete strangers in conversation. Since the airlines forbade us to read on board (they said it was a safety issue), conversation was all that staved off the boredom once the meals were served and picked up. Invariably, the chosen passenger would say, "Why are you interviewing me?" since I asked so many questions. What could a woman in this society do with these abilities?

What Can You Do for Us — Serve Coffee?

All I could imagine was myself hidden behind a large stack of books in a library somewhere, coming out occasionally to interview people, then going back to write. I had always liked to write. Where could I get a job that allowed me to do that? One day when I was exploring a magazine rack at a store near my apartment, I came across a local alternative newspaper. I called the editor and asked if he would like an article exposing the realities of life as a stewardess. He was enthusiastic, so I wrote the article, and it was promptly published.

With this success, I thought I would try to get a job with *Time* magazine, or perhaps a major newspaper. I could be a researcher and writer, I reasoned. During my days off, I started phoning news magazines and daily papers.

"Do you have any openings?" I usually began, confidently.

"Well . . . maybe . . . what is your present position?"

"I work for United Airlines."

"Oh . . ." they generally answered with a restrained, flat tone. "Doing what?"

"I'm a stewardess."

There was usually a long moment of silence, then a muffled laugh, followed by a curt or sarcastic remark like: "How did you get the idea to call *us?*" or "What do you think you could do here . . . serve coffee?"

I was hurt, but I didn't tell them about my self-analysis, disgust over how we "stews" were treated, or about feminist awakening . . . none of that. Nor did I tell them that my list started with *Time* magazine and I was working my way down from there. I was desperate and couldn't afford to sound offended, so I said with as much earnestness as I could muster: "I want to do research. I want to write."

"Yeah . . . sure . . . we don't have any openings. Sorry." Click. The calls were usually very short.

Next, I tried phoning suburban weeklies but got a similar reaction. Finally, I tried the publication on the very bottom of my list, *The Herald*, a Catholic diocesan weekly paper in a very small New Jersey town about a half hour from my apartment. I don't know if it was really his Catholic-trained politeness that made the editor actually listen to me for more than two minutes. And I really wasn't sure why this man, out of all the others who wouldn't even talk with me on the phone, wanted me to come to his office for an interview that very same day.

"How interesting! Can you come now?" he asked eagerly. "Oh," he added, in what seemed like an afterthought, "Can you bring some samples of your writing?"

"Well ... I can show you some of the papers I wrote in college and one freelance article I did recently on being a stewardess," I said.

"Okay, that's good. Bring that."

I got ready and then drove into the suburbs, parking outside the nondescript, small, one-story office building that housed the paper. It wasn't very impressive inside either, just two large rooms, a small private office for the editor, and a darkroom for the photographer. I felt a little disappointed, but, then again, there were no demanding pilots or leering passengers. There were four comfortably dressed middle-aged secretaries seated at typewriters. They looked me over and let the editor know I had arrived. It all looked really boring to me in comparison to the airlines.

I quickly figured out that this editor must have a very quiet job. It had to be a novelty for a stewardess to even appear in his offices, much less apply for a job there. I looked over the paper while I waited and saw that it covered rummage sales, bingo games, parochial schools, and church people.

Eventually the editor sent for me. He was a distinguished-looking man, probably in his early forties, wearing a navy blazer, grey wool slacks, cordovan loafers, pinstripe shirt, and an expensive, red paisley silk tie. He was obviously very well cared for and used to being fawned over. He had a glint in his eye when I came into his office. I tried to take no notice of it.

He took the folder I handed him and quickly scanned my writing. I thought he could've spent a bit more time on it, but I was pleased that he found nothing problematic. He described the job. I would have to keep up the files, write a few articles each week, do whatever the assistant editor and the photographer needed from me, such as rewrites and cut-lines, go out and interview priests, nuns, parishioners. It sounded easy enough, and, best of all, the days and hours were totally predictable. Also, I could stay on the ground.

"Okay, the writing is fine. You seem intelligent. Now, what parish do you attend?" he asked.

I had to think quickly. Obviously he was assuming that, since I had an Italian surname and was applying at his paper, I was a Catholic. But I hadn't been to church in a long time. My attendance had gradually decreased after the morning of my Virgin Mary insight in college. Becoming a feminist had clinched it, making me really ambivalent about the church. In fact, the only time I had been inside a church in the last five years was when George and I had gotten married. But I needed this job. It was the only interview I had gotten and the only chance I had to leave United Airlines.

"Uh . . . St. Peter's," I said, just picking the first saint's name that came to me.

"Peter was an important saint, wasn't he?" I mused. Surely there were St. Peter's churches everywhere. A little trickle of sweat rolled down my back, but I showed only my well-practiced, calm smile.

"Oh, yes, Parsippany, Route 46," he said, sounding satisfied. He leaned back in his swivel chair, stared at the ceiling for a minute, then abruptly sat back up and said with firm decision: "Okay. Fine. Can you start next week? The salary will be $125 a week."

"Whew—good choice of a saint—that was lucky," I thought. As for the salary, it was actually less than I had been making as a stewardess, but I didn't care. This was my only chance. The details were arranged. As a parting remark, the editor said,

smiling broadly, "Oh, by the way, you can wear your uniform to work, if you want. No need to buy any new clothes."

I had read enough feminist books by then to interpret this remark. Our one-piece mini-dress uniforms were poorly designed and rose up to mid-thigh every time we raised our arms to put luggage into the overhead bins. As the editor spoke, I noticed the high filing cabinets along the wall. That dress was the last thing I was going to wear there. Anyway, I couldn't wait to get out of it forever.

The Church Up Close

I quit United Airlines immediately and began my new job. It was good leaving for work in the morning, knowing at exactly what time I would return that afternoon. Although I had no training in journalism, I caught on quickly and found it satisfying to turn out articles that would appear in the paper just a few days later with my byline on them. I enjoyed driving around the diocese with the paper's photographer, Tom, researching stories and meeting new people. In this way I got a close look at the church, something I had only seen from the pew before.

I saw lay initiatives born of devotion to God, an engagement with the world, and a determination to make a difference. I covered stories on efforts to clean up a local polluted river, church members who helped a family with its handicapped child, and many social service efforts by congregants. I was impressed and began to enjoy the job even if it wasn't as lively as airline travel.

Many movements were burgeoning at that time, and I got to cover them. Birthright, a new Catholic anti-abortion agency, held an open house and I was sent to report on it. The opening featured a slide show of dismembered fetuses, which was obviously meant to arouse support. Afterwards, the organizers spoke to me in confident tones, assuming I agreed with them completely. I was turned off by their self-righteousness and hard-line answers. They did not know that my feminist awakening had made me skeptical of any simple solution to the problem of unwanted pregnancy. But I didn't think I could let my feelings show, so I put on a poker face, and then went back to the office and wrote up the event as objectively as I could.

The new charismatic movement—dedicated to renewal, to a closer, more personal relationship with God, and an openness to the Holy Spirit—also was stirring in the diocese. Members of this group often prayed in unintelligible languages, known as "speaking in tongues." I was sent to cover one of their prayer meetings. During the meeting, I could feel the leaders observing me closely. I had never heard "tongues" or seen people raise their arms high when they prayed. My discomfort must have showed, for I was told later that the group put me on their prayer list, figuring I was not yet filled with the Spirit. They followed up with frequent phone calls, but they never had the satisfaction of seeing me become a Catholic charismatic. Although I could see they were devout, I was offended by their presumption.

I got a new look at clergy, too. When I was a Catholic girl in Newark, priests had seemed like distant gods who deigned to notice me only to command or condescend. But now nuns and priests *had* to talk with me because they wanted us to publish their events and stories. I even got to eat with them occasionally when the editor would invite me on his almost daily lunchtime meetings with key priests and administrators. I enjoyed being treated to fancy meals in good restaurants. But it shocked me that they drank cocktails in midday during work hours and that the editor sometimes didn't go back to the office afterwards. Their talk wasn't very religious either. In fact, it seemed exceptionally political—who would succeed whom, how they could increase finances, ways *The Herald* could influence public opinion. There was a tone of cynicism that distressed me. As a sheltered ethnic girl and an enthusiastic convert, I had never seen this side of the church.

The nuns I interviewed were also different than the ones I had known previously. In my childhood they were authoritative, stern, and a bit scary. But it was post–Vatican II, and everyone was feeling freer. Many of the younger sisters no longer wore the long, enveloping black habits. Instead, they dressed in simple dark contemporary suits or dresses. Some even wore jewelry. They also began reading more widely, in such subjects as process theology and Eastern religions. One intelligent nun I interviewed gave me a copy of a book by Catholic process theologian Teilhard de Chardin, and even encouraged me to look at books from other faiths. I couldn't believe a nun would tell me to read something that was not Catholic.

Then one day I picked up the weekly paper of our chief competitor from a neighboring diocese. I noted the lead front-page article was also on the charismatic movement, something we had featured the week before. I started reading it, and, although the first paragraph was different, the rest of the article was exactly the one I had written. I was outraged and called up the reporter immediately. He was an older man who had worked there for years. He merely laughed at me and cynically remarked that there was nothing unusual about what he had done. When I complained about this to my editor at *The Herald*, he took the plagiarism philosophically, saying there was no point in doing anything about it. I was devastated that he could treat this so lightly.

After a year of looking at the church up close and trying to give it a second chance, all my disillusionments—with the political cynicism of the "in" crowd, the sometimes strident attitudes of special-interest factions, and now this blasé attitude from two different church publications toward a case of blatant plagiarism—all suddenly added up. I felt as if I had just awakened from a coma. Suddenly, all this church stuff seemed like a hoax. There was no God and all these people running around in black outfits were being duped. I was shaken to my roots. Without planning it, I had become an atheist.

Even my conversion to feminism had not pushed me into atheism. Feminism had caused some doubts regarding religion, but those ended in benign neglect of religion rather than outright rejection. It had taken an up-close look at the inner workings of the church to accomplish this. I hadn't intellectualized or planned to see the church this way. I wasn't consciously looking for flaws. Yet suddenly I found it impossible to believe in the church, religion, or even God.

This was a very destabilizing moment. It did not bring freedom or clarity. Instead, the bottom fell out of my world. Despair—something I had felt in childhood when my religious identity was in question—now returned in full force. I began to look upon priests, nuns, parishioners, and my colleagues with pity and disdain. On one hand, I envied them for having something to hang onto. On the other hand, since it was false, what good was it? Unlike my previous two conversion experiences (to Catholicism and then feminism), I didn't mention my new feelings to anyone, not even George and certainly not to anyone at *The Herald*. But I soon realized that, in good conscience, I could no longer work there.

One day, while I was covering a story in Morristown, I walked into the offices of the largest local newspaper, *The Daily Record*, and asked if they had any openings. Having worked as a reporter for a year now, I had good news clips, several awards, and relevant experience on a weekly. They offered me a job on the spot. So I returned to the Catholic paper, gave notice, and left. Finally I would become a full-fledged journalist.

George didn't seem to care one way or the other. He was still involved in getting his college degree. Between his classes and his maintenance work there, he spent a lot of time at school. One day I found multiple pictures of an unknown woman in his photography course portfolio. When I questioned him on this, I could see how uncomfortable he was. This made me suspect more was going on than he admitted. But this discovery, like the plagiarism incident, brought everything to a head for me. George and I had become increasingly alienated from each other. His chief pleasure was hanging out with his buddies, smoking and drinking. As for me, feminism had given me a larger vision, and I began to imagine a wider world for myself. But when I read books or tried to write, George took it personally, as though I were trying to be better than him.

George denied any responsibility. He figured I was the one with the problem and proposed that I see a therapist. I readily agreed since I, too, took much of the blame on myself. We had only been married a year, but everyday I realized more strongly that I had done the wrong thing. I felt terribly guilty about this. Yet it would take years for me to realize how trapped I had been, how molded into an expectation and a lifestyle that I felt duty-bound to fulfill, even if only in part.

Although I would seek more therapy in the years to come, even this initial treatment was helpful. After several months of sessions, the therapist finally said, "George can't give you what you want. Your feelings were right from the outset. You shouldn't have done it." This validation gave me courage.

Although the guilt was almost unbearable, it would be better to act now before more people got hurt. I had nightmares of his daughter running after my car crying "Mommy," but I knew I would have to admit my mistake and do something about it.

I asked George to move out. Neither of us pursued divorce very vigorously, and it would take several years before it was resolved. Nevertheless, the marriage was over. Although I was relieved, the guilt I felt at hurting him, at hurting his family, and at making my parents pay for a fancy wedding for a marriage that only lasted one year, was a heavy weight.

Backpackers and Bunnies

I loved working at *The Daily Record* immediately. This new career seemed to promise all the meaning in life I had been looking for. Even though I continued to feel guilty about my marital situation, my new life offered many compensations. All the reporters at the paper were young, idealistic, and public-spirited. We all wanted to change the world and seemed confident that we could. Since few of them were married and none had children, we had a lot of time to devote to our work. Soon we were all best friends, going out together after work (our workday lasted from 4 p.m. until midnight), usually to our favorite pub, Cutters, where we stayed until closing. Our after-hours camaraderie helped relieve the stress of covering car accidents, crime scenes, political scandals, and endless town meetings. We were inspired by the societal changes of the 1970s, and encouraged each other to use our work to help expose evil in the world and publicize goodness. Now, no longer identified with a religious organization, I felt free to uncover stories I really cared about.

It felt as if I had been born for this work. Before long, I began scoring professional successes, awards, and notice. One evening I was sent to cover the opening of a new Playboy club—a simple assignment that meant free food and an amusing article. But I snuck into the dressing room of the "bunny" waitresses and, instead, wrote an exposé of their real feelings toward the job. The editors liked it and turned it into a major feature article. The article generated many letters to the editor. The feedback, especially from our female readers, was good, although a few male letter writers made nasty remarks about me. The Playboy club, too, was incensed and lodged a formal complaint. But the publisher and editors backed me up, since generating controversy was good for the paper. Another night I was sent to the open house of a new anti-abortion agency. By this time, I felt free to write frankly about the propaganda and hard-line attitude of the movement. Again, there was protest and, again, the paper stood behind me.

My controversial stories began to generate even more letters from readers, both "for" and "against." My favorite "for" letter was from a woman who said she would be proud to call me her daughter. The editors enjoyed all the controversy and defended me publicly. The publisher was pleased, too. After all, this kind of thing sold papers.

I was coming into my own professionally. Emboldened by my success, I asked for and received five weeks of leave-time to attend a National Outdoor Leadership School wilderness survival trip. The editors thought it might make a good series. But I had other reasons, too. I wanted something dramatic to help me get over the marital breakup. I thought if I pared down life to its essentials, at least for awhile, I could figure out why I had compromised so much and how I might get over the guilt of hurting George and his family.

Also, my feminist awakening had made me want to be more active, vigorous, and strong. Although I had always swum and biked, normally I never lifted anything heavier than an overnight bag. My protective father was always rushing over, saying: "No, no, let me. You'll get a hernia like your mother." But I wanted to get strong, not merely fit. And I wanted to be brave . . . not just in big cities—where my upbringing and professional experience had made me secure—but in the wilderness, too. So I traveled to Tennessee and joined a group of young people for the trip into the wilds. At twenty-three, I was one of the oldest in this group of a dozen, roughly two-thirds of whom were teenaged boys.

My only physical preparation before leaving was to swim a few laps every day in my apartment pool. I thought that would be plenty, but the trip was a shock to my system. I had never exerted myself this much or felt in this much personal danger. The pack was nearly half my body weight, and I soon fell and sprained a knee. But when I complained about this and the many infected cuts, plus tick and chigger bites, the leader, Haven, said they'd charge me for the helicopter if they had to airlift me out. "If your knee turns green and falls off, get back to me," he said with a laugh. I cried every day and kept going.

For several weeks we backpacked, "boulder jumped," climbed, rappelled, and slept in caves, all of which were merely lessons getting us ready for the most demanding "main event," testing our abilities to survive in the wilderness. For this portion of the course, small teams of four, with no food and nothing but canoes and tents, had to make their way back to base camp over a four-day period. Each team made it back on the appointed day, exhausted and starving, but—as one final bit of hardship training—the program staff made us wait in canoes offshore while they took their time loading long tables with food. Finally, they gave a signal, and I never paddled so hard in my life. Most of us ate too fast and threw up.

Back at *The Daily Record*, even though everyone said I looked horribly thin (I had gone from about 125 pounds to about 110), I felt exultant. The whole experience had given me a physical confidence I had never had before. As promised, I wrote the series for the paper, complete with my own photos. Later that year, I won the New Jersey Press Association annual prize for Best Feature. Soon afterwards, I covered a board of education meeting in a town on my beat. The school board had announced that, in a cost-cutting measure, all school cooks and kitchens would be eliminated. Instead, they would bring in frozen "TV dinners" for the children. I organized our whole staff to interview students in the tri-county area about the quality of all types of school lunches. My series aroused parents to ask for changes, and I won First Place in Public Service Journalism from the New Jersey Press Association.

As a vote of confidence, the paper gave me my own weekly column—"Life in an Apartment"—to cover housing issues and tenants' rights. My career was going very well. When I went shopping in Morristown, people recognized me from the photo on my column. Town officials now called *me* with tips and news. My life opened up in other ways, too. The survival trip had made me want more physical vitality, so I took up jogging and bought a road bike. At that time, it was rather odd to see a grown woman doing these things in suburban New Jersey, but I continued even though leering men in cars laughed at me or tried to run me off the road. I also joined the YWCA, adopted an organic vegetarian diet, and learned all about nutritional supplements. Even my social life was wonderful. For the first time in my life, I had lots of dates and never lacked for party invitations and drinking buddies. I was the happiest I had ever been.

Spiritual Longing

Yet something inside me knew all of this would never be enough, no matter how many front-page articles I had, how many prizes I won, how many guys wanted to date me, or how fit I could become. The vacuum created by my de-conversion from the church had not been filled by my career success and active life. I didn't know it then, but I had a spiritual emptiness at my core that nothing else could fill but God. Later I would learn that I was having a visceral experience of what St. Augustine meant when he said "Our hearts are restless until they rest in Thee." So, without a conscious plan, I began to try more specifically spiritual alternatives. I was edging away from atheism and back toward agnosticism.

I began to comb bookstores again and found a copy of the Bhagavad Gita, a book the nun from my religious reporting days had recommended. I couldn't quite understand it, but something there filled me with longing. Soon I started attending yoga classes and was attracted to the vitality of my teacher, Trudy Zappe. I arranged to interview her for the local alternative paper, and followed her advice on diet and exercise.

I joined the Integral Yoga Institute, met Swami Satchidananda, became an informal member of an ashram, and went on many yoga retreats. The people were sincere, the program was well organized, the food was interesting, and the exercises felt good—although the cleansing techniques, like swallowing one end of a rag and bringing up whatever it absorbed—went a little too far for me. In fact, so bodily and internally focused seemed all their spiritual concerns that I began to grow impatient, anxious to direct more of my attention outward. Although other adherents seemed satisfied, I found that their philosophy and methods did not help me with my growing disquiet over the nuclear arms race or ecological destruction. Neither did the ashram give me a place to discuss the ongoing internal conflict caused by my mixed-faith background. There were many members who had Jewish backgrounds, but they didn't want to explore the differences between these two spiritualities. Just as dismaying, the ashram members seemed immune to my concerns about women's rights.

One day when I was in the local health food store, a young American yoga teacher, clad in white robes, recognized me from class. Seeing me crouching down to get something off a lower shelf, he came over, silently reached down and applied his warm palm to the top of my head. I looked up with surprise and said, "Oh ... uh ... Hi!" Saying nothing, he simply smiled benevolently down at me and moved on. The touch of his warm hand on my head reminded me of the priest in Newark who had supposed that his blessing on my head would substitute for a hat in church. I stayed there another moment or two and had another one of my sudden blinding moments of clarity. I realized that I might not yet know what I *did* need to attain spiritual fulfillment, but what I definitely *didn't* need to rely on anymore was someone else's pats and hats!

After the inaction of the ashram, I wanted more political involvement. Ecology particularly interested me, so I joined Zero Population Growth. Here were people who cared about the earth. But one evening an older woman suggested we send letters to all new parents. We could search out birth announcements in the paper and let them know they were responsible for overpopulating the earth. Her face was tense and her voice bitter as she suggested this activity. I was disquieted and quit the group.

One day I got into a conversation with a woman in the

sauna at the YWCA. She suggested I try a movement called "Unity." She explained that the group had helped her develop a more positive attitude toward life. She said people of many different religious backgrounds joined it. Back at the lockers, she gave me a pamphlet and suggested I visit her minister. As I understood it from the literature, the Unity philosophy espoused certain attitudinal changes as an end to emptiness and inner turmoil. I went to visit the Unity minister, who confirmed that the movement could help me in my spiritual searchings.

I tried hard to follow the minister's guidelines, reading the devotional literature and meditating. The Unity minister met with me weekly, and, as suggested, each time I would give her a check for ten percent of my pay—she called it a "tithe." She said that tithing would help me be more committed. I was unfamiliar with this concept, and it felt like a significant sum for no clear reason. Nor could I understand how becoming more peaceful inside could help with external problems like the gas crisis, unequal rights for women, or the threat of nuclear war. I didn't last more than three months in Unity.

Knowing I was now an avid seeker, other friends also began inviting me to their own spiritual favorites, such as Erhard Seminars Training, which was commonly known as *est.* A colleague said she was getting much peace from meditating and I should try Transcendental Meditation (TM). I was all signed up to attend my first class and receive my mantra when my car broke down just as I was about to leave. Dori—a fellow reporter and former Catholic who had become an evangelical Christian in college—told me darkly that there was a reason why I should not go, and I should give up all plans to try TM. I thought this was weird, but I never went back to the group.

The Problem with Jeff

I probably would have kept trying different things and staying on at the newspaper for many more years—except for Jeff. On my first day at the job, the editor had seated me opposite a young, bearded, hippy-looking reporter, introducing him as "Jeff, from Michigan." Jeff didn't say much at first, but his appearance intrigued me, as did his habit of flashing the peace sign to anyone who walked into the office. *"Wow, a real radical,"* I thought.

Jeff could see I was inexperienced in secular journalism. He took it upon himself to help me adjust to my new job. He also realized I was especially vulnerable because of the marital dissolution, which I soon told him about at great length. Perhaps this gave him confidence to pursue me. In any case, before long we realized we were attracted to each other. We had one important thing in common. Like me, Jeff was a disillusioned ex-Catholic. However, he had the advantage of a Catholic education, even studying with the rigorous Jesuits at college, so he knew religion from the inside. Here, finally, was someone I could discuss my spiritual explorations with. Yet each time I came up with a new technique or group, he would insist I was naïve and disparage my attempts, showing how they were intellectual dead-ends.

My fellow reporters saw that I was spending a lot of time with Jeff, and they became concerned. They tried to warn me that Jeff was troubled and difficult. They related how he would argue with them for no reason, how he would abruptly break off a conversation and run out into the night, forgetting even to take his coat. They said he was so obsessed with cleanliness that he wiped down his entire apartment with PhisoHex. Their warnings troubled me, but I was very attracted to Jeff's intelligence. I could talk with him about anything, and he often surprised me with his insights. In addition, I was still getting over the marital breakup and appreciated Jeff's listening ear. He took me seriously and seemed to want me to be happy. However, just as my colleagues warned me, Jeff had his odd side, too. He started following me all around the office as I worked, which was endearing—for a little while. But soon, it became worrisome. I would try to be clear with him that his attentions were too much for an office environment, but if anything this made him worse. I suppose that I may have rationalized it early on as the normal persistence of a male who really liked a female. After all, weren't guys *supposed* to be persistent when they liked someone? It was just one of the gender rules—and, anyway, I was flattered.

When he was promoted to night editor, and thus became my boss, there was no way I could avoid his increasingly insistent attentions. Finally, when Jeff moved to an apartment near mine and started showing up unexpectedly at all the places I frequented—the laundromat, the coffee shop, the gas station—I became concerned. When he told me late one night on the phone that I had "touched his brain" and was now "responsible" for him, I decided I'd better end it. But although I kept breaking up with him, Jeff kept pursuing me.

Leave of Absence

Jeff was not the only problem. As time wore on and I got used to the newspaper business, I began to worry that reporting was not a good job for an older person. We all felt sorry for the one reporter in our office who was over forty. Although editing would have been a logical next step, it didn't appeal to me. I didn't want to be stuck behind a desk for the rest of my life.

One event brought me to another of my moments when

random insights suddenly turn into decision. A bunch of us from *The Daily Record* attended the State Press Association awards dinner. My friends and the whole banquet hall broke out into wild applause when my name was announced as the first-place winner for Public Service Journalism. But as I went up to claim my plaque, the applause hardly registered with me. Instead, I kept hearing the Peggy Lee song running through my mind: "Is that all there is?"

I didn't know what to make of this. Perhaps a new job would help me find relief. I thought maybe television news or a more prestigious paper might be a satisfying goal. So I applied for a job at a larger paper, *The Bergen Record*, closer to Manhattan and considered a "farm team" for *The New York Times*. When they offered me the job, I asked if I could start in a few months and, surprisingly, they agreed. I knew I needed to take a break first. But where could I go to guarantee I would have the space and time to think things through? The wilderness expedition had been too difficult to give me the luxury to re-evaluate my life. I wanted someplace where I would automatically feel happy and relaxed. To me the answer was obvious: Italy.

Italy Is the Answer

All my life I had heard my Italian relatives talk about "the old country." They would minimize the poverty and stress the beauty, culture, and food. Whenever Italian opera was broadcast on the radio, my father and uncle would turn it up loud as they worked in the back of the shop. When I expressed displeasure, they would insist it was the best music in the world. According to my family, no one was as beautiful as Sophia Loren, as great as Pavarotti, as important to America as Columbus, or as handsome as Marcello

Mastroianni. Holiday dinner conversations often revolved around the superiority of Italian culture, music, products, and foods.

For instance, Uncle Amedeo might hold up his glass and say, "This wine is Italian, sure, but it isn't like we have in the old country. They don't send the good stuff here."

My Aunt Marietta would take me aside and show me a bracelet or pin made in Italy. "Look at this, Linda. Isn't this beautiful. It's eighteen caret. Here the gold is only fourteen caret and sometimes even ten. Don't be fooled. Make sure your parents get you the real thing," she would say confidentially.

My cousin Anna might chime in that Italian leather goods were far superior to American. She might even display a wallet, purse, or gloves as an example. Her husband, Rob, would rhapsodize about each meal they had eaten on their latest trip overseas, describing the menu exactly.

In the midst of this, my father would often remark that America was a good country, and they had been poor in Italy. There would be the usual choruses of "Sure, sure, this is the best country in the world," and then everyone would go back to explaining how the food was better over there, the culture more refined, the styles more stylish, the people more gracious. These conversations provided me with a clear philosophy: life in America was crass and boorish. Only in Italy could one really live with grace and style. I had grown up thinking that if only I could get to Italy, life would be beautiful.

And, indeed, life had been beautiful there the one time I had visited—a whirlwind two-week tour with my parents and brother right after my college graduation. I had felt relaxed, happy, and connected in Italy. Suddenly, all I wanted was to go back. And to get away from *The Daily Record*, from Jeff, and from my futile searchings for a spiritual home. Also, the country was feeling increasingly chaotic—the gas crisis had been the latest in a series of unsettling events. Because of it, I had to get up very early and wait in long lines at the pump. Sitting there in the dim light, I felt worried about the country's future. This would be a good time to leave.

So I gave notice at *The Daily Record*, canceled my magazine subscriptions, gave away my furniture, moved out of my apartment, and left my car with the family. I bought the cheapest ticket I could find—arrival and departure out of Luxembourg, with an open return date, good for one year. I intended to hitchhike south until I got to Italy—other than that, I had no plan. Although it was sad to leave my friends at the paper, I received only encouragement.

"Wow, I envy you. I wish I were that brave," said several of my peers.

"This is the time to do it, now while you're young," said my older friends, wistfully.

There were several going-away parties for me—the largest given by Dori—my evangelical Christian friend who had discouraged me from trying TM. I spent the last few days before my flight at her house, which proved a smart move. Dori had known Jeff since they were in college together and had always warned me to stay away from him. As my departure date got closer, he began to act more strangely, showing up at her door, shouting up at our windows, insisting she send me out to talk with him. But instead she kept ordering him to leave, threatening to call the police.

In her new role as my protector, Dori also thought the moment was ripe for some evangelization. She started by offering me some reading material, several books by her favorite Christian evangelist, Dr. Francis Schaeffer, a Protestant minister who headed up L'Abri, a retreat center in Switzerland. I returned them with an apology, saying I did not want to add heavy things to my small pack. She countered by suggesting that I visit the community once I arrived in Europe. I didn't pay much attention to what she said about them or their philosophy. Instead, I assumed it was just some kind of commune in a beautiful setting. It didn't matter anyway. I had no more interest in anyone's pet spiritualities.

I did listen, however, when Dori said they that would take in anyone, had minimal fees, and didn't require anything except some manual labor. She gave me a hand-drawn map of its location, "just in case," she said. I tucked it away in my pack, thinking I just might drop in there if I got tired of hitchhiking. I was a good worker, as spiritual as the next person, I figured, and familiar with retreats from my yoga experience.

I was filled with relief when my preparations were completed and the day of my flight came. I boarded the plane for Europe with just a few hundred dollars, a backpack, a sleeping bag, and little else. It was early April and I didn't even bother to bring a coat.

Chapter Six

Finding God in Switzerland

Close Calls

It was cold, wet, and dreary when I landed in Luxembourg. In order to sleep off my jet lag, I immediately searched for a cheap hotel, trudging through the gray streets with my backpack. The only other backpacker I saw that day was a young American whining that her bag was too heavy. I helped her carry it awhile and wondered if I seemed as out of place as she did—I who had just given up everything, my job, my friends, my apartment, even my furniture (although at that moment I couldn't quite remember why).

The hotel room I found was run-down and barren, with its metal bed, chipped porcelain sink, and bare floor. The next morning, after the hotel's hard roll and coffee, I went in search of a youth hostel. Besides feeling generally wretched, I couldn't afford to waste my money on hotel rooms. I had brought only $500, and it had to last. There was no way I was going to ask my parents to send me money. They already thought I was crazy to leave my job and the country.

At the hostel I had some good luck. In the upper bunk was a thirty-year-old American named Karen, about five years older than I, and a former Army nurse recently discharged after serving in Germany. She was ready to celebrate and have some adventures before taking a hospital job she had lined up in Boston. In the meantime, her only plans were to meet up with a girlfriend in Switzerland in a few weeks for some traveling.

"I'm just going to be hitchhiking around," I said. "Would you like to go together?"

"Good idea," she said enthusiastically. "We can protect each other on the road, and it will be great to have a partner." She seemed mature, strong, and reliable.

Karen and I were on the road the next morning right after the hostel's scanty breakfast of bread and coffee. Our first ride was in a truck with two men wearing the blue overalls of manual laborers. The driver put our packs in the open back and then motioned for us to join them on the bench seat in front. Before we knew it, we were speeding down the road with Karen squeezed in next to the driver and me on the other one's lap. The men began laughing and pawing us. After several miles we told them we had come to our destination.

They pulled over and stopped the truck but took hold of us, saying they would not return our bags unless we kissed them. While Karen wrestled with the driver, I reached underneath his partner's arm and slammed down on the door handle. The door opened, I jumped out and grabbed our bags. This distracted them enough that Karen was able to extricate herself. As the men drove off, we looked at each other and started laughing. "No more trucks!" we said simultaneously.

The next couple of rides were fine—middle-aged European couples in respectable sedans. The last ride dropped us off on a quiet stretch of back road. It was lunchtime and we were really hungry. After about a half-hour, two young Italian men in a shiny black Fiat convertible stopped for us. Karen and I consulted briefly, noting that we could sit together with our packs in the back seat.

We drove for a few miles and then the guys stopped at a

small village. While we waited, they went into a shop, and came out with a bottle of wine, a large loaf of bread, and several small packages wrapped in oily white paper. With my fairly minimal Italian, I understood them to say that we would now have a picnic lunch. This sounded good to us— we had seen lots of people having lovely picnics, tablecloth and all, beside the road.

"*This is just so European*," I thought with pleasure as we sped off again, my long curly hair whipping into my eyes and mouth, and dirt flying into my contact lenses. Still, everything was working out so well. After driving awhile, the guys pulled off into a meadow, far from the road, and spread out a blanket. They motioned for us to sit down and eat. From the tiny trunk they brought out utensils, glasses, and a corkscrew.

Things were fine until all the food and wine was gone. Then they abruptly stood up, each grabbed one of us and motioned that we should now take a walk. I stood frozen, not knowing what to do. But Karen started yelling, flailing, and protesting. Her actions roused me, and I combined pathetic Italian and frantic English to say people were waiting for us and we didn't have time. The guys fought with us for awhile, but, finally disgusted, they threw our packs on the ground and drove off.

For the first time, I realized that living "on the edge" might not be as appealing as I had envisioned. Karen and I walked back to the road and continued our trip. After several days of this—some good rides and some close calls, spending the nights in cold, uncomfortable youth hostels—Karen decided we needed to go straight to her friend's house in a small suburb of Geneva.

The next day we arrived in the village mid-morning. Her friend's mother met us at the door with a cocktail in her hand. She seemed to be expecting us and invited us in, insisting we have a vodka and tonic with her. I had never drunk alcohol in the morning before, and it began to make me feel woozy. But I snapped out of it when I saw how upset Karen was to learn that her friend had gotten tired of waiting. The mother explained, in heavily accented English, that her daughter had already left to begin the trip they had planned and would wait for Karen at a certain hotel.

Karen decided to take a train to her friend immediately. Although she invited me, I could not afford the expense. Besides, I still wanted to hitchhike around some more. So, sadly, I accompanied Karen to the train station in Geneva, where we said a final good-bye. As we stood on the platform, she rummaged around in her backpack, and said: "Here, I want you to take my turtleneck." She handed me a burgundy wool sweater. "You're going to be cold here in Switzerland. You don't even have a coat."

I wanted to cry. Suddenly this adventure didn't seem so much fun anymore. After the train pulled out, I walked over to the station café to have a cup of coffee and refocus. Searching in my pack for a map of Switzerland, I came across the hand-drawn map to the retreat center in Switzerland that Dori had given me. Comparing the two maps, I realized that the place she had recommended was not too far. Surely I could hitchhike there in a day if I got lucky with rides. Dori had said they would take anyone and let them stay as long as they liked. By now I was definitely ready to stay in one place for awhile. I went back on the road and stuck out my thumb.

I had no trouble getting rides and quickly pieced together several in the right direction. My last ride was with an old Italian guy in a racy red two-seat Alfa Romeo. The man looked about seventy-five and seemed delighted to have a passenger. Between my minimal Italian and his barebones English, we managed to establish quite a lot: he would take me right up to the door of L'Abri; but first, because the day was still young, he would conduct some business in the next village while I had lunch; then we would rendezvous. He even gave me the money for my lunch and dropped me off at an attractive restaurant along the lake. I felt weird accepting this from him, but I really wanted the ride, so I stayed there until he came back an hour later.

The old man seemed surprised and happy that I was still there. As he loaded my things back into his car, I had a sense of dread, wondering if he would try to get some kind of repayment. As we drove along, I strategized on how I would get out of various likely situations. Fortunately, the man's best effort was simply to keep pulling the car over on the pretext of seeing the views, and then try to kiss me. "*Wow,*" I thought with some admiration, "*these Italians never give up!*" I felt ashamed that I had let myself get into this just for a ride and lunch. But the situation was easy to handle; he wasn't very strong when he pushed against me; and when I pushed back, his old-fashioned manners made him back off.

Fattened for the Kill

Eventually, we pulled up in front of a large chalet that appeared to be the main building among a small gathering of houses. Before I could grab my pack and get out, this aging Italian playboy smiled broadly, pulled down the neck of my shirt, and stuffed some francs into my bra. After I got out, he blew me a kiss, squealed his wheels, and sped off down the mountain road. "*Okay, so it wasn't a total loss for him,*" I thought. "*He probably doesn't have experiences like this very often anymore, Italian or not, and he can tell his friends about it.*"

Suddenly, though, I looked up and saw that all the front windows of the chalet faced this driveway. "*What if someone inside saw this?*" I thought, feeling embarrassed as I walked

up the short path. I didn't even have a chance to knock before the front door opened and there stood an American
who introduced himself as Rick. He didn't look a bit surprised to see me, acting as if it were perfectly natural to get
such unexpected visitors.

"Welcome to L'Abri," he said, and led me into a small reception room. Since the large chalet seemed deserted, I
asked where everyone was.

"Oh, they're all down at a communion service," Rick said.

"*Uh oh,*" I thought, "*that sounds kind of religious. Maybe I
should have paid more attention to what Dori was trying to tell me
about this place.*"

Rick explained that they didn't have room for me right
now in a chalet—it seemed they owned quite a few houses
in this small village and could accommodate many visitors—
but if I would stay at Madame Ruchet's *dortoir,* or attic dormitory, down the hill, soon they would make room for me as
a student.

"Just walk down towards the cow barn there. When you
smell the manure pile, turn left," he said. "You'll find it."

Soon I had a bed in an attic with several other young
women, all waiting for student slots. "*Wait a minute,*" I thought
after getting settled. "*What does he mean by 'student'? I just
want a place to stay for a few days or a week.*" I walked back
to the large chalet, which he had told me was called Les
Mélèzes. It seemed that all the chalets had names. I marched
in and told Rick I had no intention of studying anything and
maybe I should go. He seemed concerned and suggested we
go for a walk together. Before we set out, he said: "You look
cold. Don't you have a coat? Didn't you know that it's always
much colder up here in the mountains?"

I told him I hadn't brought one from the States and hadn't
planned on coming here. I told him about my friend Dori,
who had been here several years ago, and he remembered

her. Then a kind of a knowing look passed over his face. "Oh . . . so *Dori* told you to come here . . . but she didn't tell you much about this place? Ohhhh . . . Okay," he said confidently and smiled. Then he told me to wait, went up some stairs, and came back with a nondescript old navy blue nylon parka, only just a bit too big for me.

"You can keep this," he said. "It's from the grab bag."

"What's that?" I asked.

"Oh, people leave stuff they don't need anymore, and those who need things take them. No charge. No problem. You can get some interesting things up there," he added.

I was touched by his thoughtfulness. With Karen's turtleneck on and the coat from this guy, I felt much better. It seemed amazing that suddenly I was being given things I needed without even asking—a sweater, lunch, money, a parka. Rick and I tromped along for nearly an hour on the dirt paths around the village. He asked me about my background, my upbringing, and my beliefs. He seemed especially interested in my mixed-faith parentage and my spiritual searchings. After a few interchanges, I began to get the picture. *"Damn,"* I thought. *"This is just another one of those places where they empty you out so they can fill you up with their stuff. Damn."*

Before we arrived back at the chalet, Rick said he suddenly remembered there was a vacant bed at Beau Site, a nearby chalet. I should go back to the bed-and-breakfast, he said, get my stuff, and move right in. I was glad I didn't have to pay for a place to stay, but I was suspicious that he had suddenly made room for me. *"I must be a hot prospect,"* I thought cynically. But I was tired and the old Italian man had been the last straw. I didn't want to hit the road again for a while. *"Okay,"* I thought. *"I can go along with this. What could it hurt to stay here for a few days?"*

Soon I was wandering around, observing the scene, and

enjoying the mountains. I also began attending the lectures, which were in English. Many of them were given by Francis Schaeffer, the head of L'Abri. I soon learned that Francis Schaeffer was an American minister from the conservative Reformed Presbyterian denomination. With his wife, Edith, he had started L'Abri as a mission to disaffected youth. After a meager beginning, L'Abri had become a bustling place, with almost a hundred students, plus an extensive set of other leaders and "helpers." Most were American, along with some British, Australians, New Zealanders, and Indians. Everywhere I went, I saw people conversing intently with one another. I heard people refer to Dr. Schaeffer all the time and quote from his many books, which could conveniently be purchased in the bookshop. Many of his writings referred to the intellectual and spiritual decline of Western culture.

While Francis controlled the intellectual aspect of L'Abri, Edith worked on its hospitality. At mealtimes every effort was made to provide a gracious setting that would facilitate intense but civilized conversation. Tables were beautifully laid with tablecloths, fabric napkins, flowers, and even candles. The pace was leisurely, and proper serving protocols were followed. There was no grabbing food, boisterousness, or interrupting allowed. Instead, everyone sat up straight, stayed in their seats, and politely contributed to the conversation. It was so unlike the fun-loving, light-hearted, less restrained family meals I had enjoyed at home. Nevertheless, I was impressed with the intellectual tone of the whole thing.

But the food was something else. While it was Switzerland outside, inside at the table it was the Protestant Midwest. After my ethnic background and my recent love affair with health foods, this was my worst culinary nightmare. Here was how the "real white people" ate. I also realized later that finances played a large part in determining the L'Abri menu:

the need to feed hordes of people on what was basically a scanty "mission" budget. We had cereal and white bread for breakfast. Lunch was bean soup, yogurt, and more white bread. Dinner featured starchy casseroles, a few cooked vegetables if they were in season, lots of potatoes, rice—and more bread. With so many people sharing, seconds were rarely available—except for bread. On Sunday, if we were lucky, we might get a boiled egg in the morning and a chicken wing for dinner. Actually, I noted immediately, it was the girls who got the wings while the boys got the legs or breast meat. We had fruit only infrequently, and the only snack food allowed was the leftover bread.

I was hungry all the time, especially for protein. But instead, I ate bread . . . and dessert. I had never been a dessert fan before, but here I ate it out of necessity. I also ate the Swiss chocolate that students often passed around in study hall. As a result, I began to gain weight. My jeans became increasingly tight and uncomfortable, but I had no spare funds either to balance my diet or to buy new clothes (and the grab bag had its limits). No wonder the guys called L'Abri "the place of the fat chicks."

It didn't take long before I noted that the women did all the traditional domestic chores and largely stayed inside, while the guys got to work outdoors, or teach classes, pray at meals, and generally run things. This annoyed me, yet— fresh from my consciousness-raising groups in the U.S.—I had a thought: "*Maybe I have a purpose here. I can help awaken these women to their true situation.*" Obviously, feminism had not yet reached the Alps. I set to work immediately. I visited community women as they ironed, made beds, and cooked. I got a mixed reaction as I worked on my feminist agenda. A few thought I had a point, but in the end, they always said this structure was "biblical." I soon realized that liberating these women was going to be a difficult task. Yet I was encouraged when a student said to me: "Ever since you came, everyone is talking about women's roles here."

It was clear, however, that nothing would change unless the leadership did. So, at the public lectures I began raising questions, in my acerbic East Coast journalistic manner, challenging the leaders. No one, especially Dr. Schaeffer, appreciated this. At first he tried to answer my questions with what I felt were pat remarks, quoting the Bible with a tone of finality. Finally at one evening meeting, when I would not accept what he said, he lost his cool and pronounced loudly: "This is what's wrong with your generation. You have no authority structure. We're talking about the *Word of God* here! This is True Truth."

"Well, I don't believe in it," I said angrily.

A Jewel in Someone's Crown

I stayed, though. I could eat and sleep here for free. More important, I found the people intriguing. On one hand, I was appalled by the many Schaeffer "wannabes": mostly young guys emulating the leader's tone of voice, pronouncements, and even the knickers that Francis Schaeffer wore every day except Sunday, when he appeared in a black preacher's suit. But there were others who seemed exceptionally wise and mature. I was most struck by their pervasive sense of joy and peace. They seemed so confident and purposeful.

Dori had not told me L'Abri was evangelical Protestant, or maybe I had not heard her. Back at *The Daily Record* I had known that Dori was once a Catholic but now professed to be "a Christian." At the time I did not know (and probably would not have cared) that this was how evangelicals distinguished themselves from "liberals" and others outside the fold. While I liked Dori as a friend, I did not want to hear anything about her stay at L'Abri or about her conversion. So I was unprepared for the line of thinking here at L'Abri. Once I began to listen to them, however, their criticisms of America resonated with my 1970s "question authority" mentality. And I was struck by their nostalgic insistence that America had been on a downward slide ever since the Enlightenment. At the time, I could not clearly distinguish the difference between this backward-looking societal critique and the more forward-looking societal critique I had picked up in America in the late 1960s and early 70s. I equated their hippie clothes, long hair, and sense of community with the superficially similar youth culture from back home—and began to warm to them. Yet when I tried to maintain my journalistic interest in current events—frequently trudging up the mountain road to Villars to purchase newspapers and magazines—the leaders insisted that the only knowledge I really needed was contained in the Bible.

But the leaders impressed me with their thoughtful and (usually) kind approach. For even though I was argumentative and sometimes hostile, they took me and my concerns seriously. They responded intelligently and even praised me for asking such good questions. In addition, they seemed to care about ecology, they practiced sustainable farming, and they treated each other as family. Most of the things I had been taught about Protestants by my two sides of the family—that they are cold, distant, not relational, inhospitable—these people seemed to contradict.

The real clincher was that they considered my Jewish background an advantage, rather than a handicap. Here were the first Christians I had ever met who did not seem anti-Semitic. In fact, they said I was more fortunate than they. For they were only "spiritual Jews," grafted in, while I was the real thing, original. Actually, these people seemed to like Jews a whole lot more than they liked Catholics, whom they felt were mired in their Roman mistakes about the pope, priests, and the Eucharist being real body and blood. We didn't need saints, they said—we were all saints. We didn't need intermediaries between us and God, they said—the church was "the priesthood of believers." We didn't need priests to tell us what to believe—we could read the Bible for ourselves.

Teachings such as these appealed to me: that I might be as good as any saint; that I didn't need a priest to approach God; that I could read Scripture for myself. And, best of all, according to these Protestants, Jews were not automatically going to hell. In fact, they actually expected that many Jews would eventually "see the light"—at least by the time that Jesus came back. And in the end we'd all be together in heaven. They had no trouble with my mixed parentage but thought it was "a sign" that I was sent here by God. If I accepted Jesus as the Messiah, they said, I would be a "completed Jew." To them, this was even better than being a regular Christian.

Much later I learned that all this came from their belief system of "premillenial dispensationalism"—a theology that arranged God's revelations into an ordered series of steps, culminating in the end times—which would be heralded by widespread conversion of the Jews. Obviously finding a Jew at their door helped confirm their sense that Jesus would be coming back soon. I fit right into their plan. If someone managed to convert me, I'd become another jewel in their heavenly crown.

But I didn't want to be a notch in anybody's belt. I didn't want to give them the satisfaction of "winning" me. And their way of being a Christian seemed to mean I would have to accept their ideas on gender, that men were rightfully in control, and women rightfully subordinate. Not to mention the bland food, Midwestern sensibilities, and the catchy phrases Dr. Schaeffer was prone to (such as "True Truth" and "push them to the logic of their presuppositions"). Would I, a journalist appreciative of American liberalism, soon, like them, be making pious pronouncements on the sorry state of the world ever since the Enlightenment?

Then again, they proselytized in a way much more respectful than some other groups I had encountered. They seemed to care about the state of my soul and, equally important, my mind. And the things they said about good, evil, truth, God—and even many of the things they said about the Jews—made sense to me. Life was not meaningless. Our deepest longings were not irrational but put there for a reason. They testified to a good God and a divine plan for everyone who would accept it.

The struggle inside me went on for many weeks, as two conflicting forces vied. I kept my feelings to myself, though, only discussing them with one or two of the other "unbelieving" students. The most disturbing moment came when Evelyn, a musician from California and my best friend there, said sadly to me over a glass of wine at the village pub: "I'm afraid it's true, Linda. I think they may be right about God and all that." "*Oh, no, not Evelyn,*" I thought. "*Damn.*" The two of us had heard every lecture Dr. Schaeffer gave, listened to instructional tapes in the library, argued at mealtimes with the leaders, and had scoffed at their conservative gender ideas. But some of the things we heard there had drawn us in. So we debated privately about whether we had to buy their whole program. Could we believe in God, become Christians, and yet keep our liberal views?

The Bible and the Chosen People

After I was there about a month, someone gave me my own copy of the Bible. Rather than giving me a Scofield Reference Bible—one of the favored versions at L'Abri and the primer of dispensational theology—they gave me a contemporary translation which, I guess, they thought would be easier for me to understand. Their suspicions of Catholicism were confirmed when I told them that I had never even held a Bible before. My parents did not own one, nor did the priests encourage laypersons to interpret Scripture for themselves. So all I knew of the Bible were the verses I had heard at mass and—because this was before school prayer was outlawed—during morning "exercises" in public school.

I was at a real disadvantage at L'Abri. Everybody else seemed to know their Bibles almost by heart, whereas I hardly knew which books were "Old Testament" and which were "New." The leaders at L'Abri suggested I start with the Book of John. But, given my lack of knowledge, I decided to begin at the beginning, Genesis, and work forward. When I got to the Book of Isaiah, and to the account of the travail and exile of the Jews, suddenly I felt history walking across these pages. "So," I thought with a shock, "the Jews really are the Chosen People!" I had thought they just said that to make themselves feel better because people were prejudiced against them. After several weeks of reading, I began to feel the lifelong fog caused by my mixed background begin to clear. Things began making sense. The two halves of the Bible (Old Testament and New Testament), Jesus' Jewishness, the whole thing. My background wasn't mixed up; it was cohesive. It was the same God, the same faith. I didn't have to feel torn apart. I was whole.

On Sunday after I had this insight, I was invited to lunch at the apartment of a middle-aged American couple from Colorado, Lois and Perry Ball, who were studying at L'Abri for several months. Since he was a doctor, they could afford to rent their own apartment up the road from the center. I knew the food would be plentiful and I would get some meat. Lois confided later that she was "a little scared" of me at first, sensing anger and hostility. Yet she and her husband both treated me with respect, taking very seriously my questions about gender. Soon Lois warmed to me, saying: "You remind me of myself when I was your age. Feisty, independent."

During our meal together, we again discussed my fears about Christianity and gender. After listening to me, they pulled out their Bible and read Galatians 3:28, which asserts that "in Christ there is no Jew or Greek, slave or free, male or female." In other words, they said, I could be free as a woman and still be a Christian. Not only that, but they reiterated what I had been hearing from the leaders: I was very special to have both a Jewish and Christian heritage. And, in Christ, I would not give up my Jewish side but, instead, find it confirmed and brought to fruition.

So . . . I did not have to repudiate anything. In my Catholic conversion I had felt forced to choose between my two sides. In my feminist conversion, my trust in God had come under scrutiny. And when I had seen that God's followers—the church—were fallible, I had been shocked into atheism. But now I could see that all of me—Jewish, Christian, and female—was good in God's eyes.

I felt safe with these two; they had no institutional agenda and nothing to gain. So—as casually as I could manage—I asked what one did if one wanted to invite Jesus in. With characteristic Protestant restraint, as though this was an everyday occurrence, Lois told me to close my eyes and repeat after her: "Lord Jesus, please come into my heart, forgive my sins, and make me your own." I did this, and when I raised my head, Lois was staring at me and beaming. "You're a Christian now," she said with a broad smile. Then the two of them hugged me and sent me out into the night, back to my own chalet.

Angel Rockettes

"That's it?" I thought as I walked down the steep path back to the village. The leaders had told me all the angels in heaven rejoice when someone accepts Christ, so I half expected to see something dramatic in that clear alpine sky— maybe some angel Rockettes dancing. But nothing happened. Where was *my* sign? Even so, I felt deeply satisfied, as if I had just eaten a good meal after a long fast. In the next few days, I began to realize I had experienced a profound conversion, reaching more deeply inside me than my previous ones.

But I told no one at L'Abri about my decision for weeks. I just wanted to be sure this was the real thing, not some coerced confession or a phony effort on my part to fit in. And I guess I also didn't want to give any of the leaders the satisfaction that they had "won." I was still worried that I would have to agree to be subordinate now. In the meantime, I finally started getting what I felt were the signs from God I had been seeking, signs that made my heart feel, like John Wesley's, "strangely warmed": a letter from a journalist friend, saying she had become a Christian; a card from Dori saying she would come visit; finding things in the grab bag that I really needed.

But most important, certain Bible passages began to "jump" out at me, such as the one written by the apostle Paul, himself a converted Jew: "I have become all things to all people, that I might by all means save some" (1 Corinthians 9:22). So maybe, I thought, there was a purpose in my mixed background and wide spiritual seekings. Maybe it was my job to understand, empathize, and reach out to many different types of people. At last I was starting to feel my life had real meaning, that nothing had been wasted.

Eventually I began to let on that I had accepted Christ. As I expected, there was some sense of satisfaction in the leaders, but also happiness and celebration. Now I didn't mind so much that they could chalk me up as one more convert—lots of my friends there were also coming to the same decision. It seemed everyone was becoming a Christian. But this time my conversion did more than rearrange the way the world looked to me. Instead, it seemed to rearrange *me*. For the first time, I felt as if the two disparate parts of me had been bound together the way the Old and New Testaments were bound together in one book. I identified with Jesus and felt whole in him.

Yet I also felt I had been freer in making this choice than any of my previous ones. In fact, as I learned from these Protestant evangelicals, it was all about choice.

According to them, conversion was a conscious decision. You couldn't be born to it, like Judaism. Nor was any priestly action required. And only *you* were able to recognize that God was calling. But unlike many other students, I had not come to L'Abri feeling a need to be "saved." I wasn't really worried about going to hell—I had lost that fear when I became Catholic. Of course, I knew sin was a reality. My inherited Jewish sense of guilt was still fully functioning. And my years of Catholic confession gave me a definite awareness of my shortcomings. But I also had a strong assurance of God's pardon. My issue wasn't an unforgiving God. I simply thought something must be especially wrong with *me*. At L'Abri, I was encouraged to learn that *all* had sinned and fallen short of the glory of God. This new perspective explained a lot of things. So even though my needs didn't fit exactly into the language used by the L'Abri people, somehow I understood that these needs would be met by God.

Liberals and Women

The one thing everyone seemed to agree on at L'Abri was that the world was "going to hell in a handbasket," whatever that meant. According to Schaeffer, society was breaking down, falling further and further away from some ideal time when Western civilization was Christian. "The liberals have taken over the church and they don't even believe in the divinity of Jesus Christ," one leader said during a seminar.

Their view of liberalism puzzled me. I had always thought being "liberal" was a good thing. Here I was told, instead, that liberals were actually our archenemies and false Christians. I should be very careful what church I attended back in the States, they said.

While my fears about environmental disaster, racial conflict, and governmental corruption seemed to fit right in with this group's apocalyptic views, my feminism did not. They viewed feminism as yet one more sign of societal breakdown; I viewed feminism as a solution, not a problem. To me feminism had been fresh air and sunshine. I couldn't reconcile my strong gut instinct about gender-equality with the sex-discrimination of these otherwise caring people. When I read the Bible, the gospel spoke liberation to me, not subordination.

One Sunday evening, Mack, the leader of our chalet asked everyone to gather in the living room because some of the students had a surprise. This wasn't unusual since, without television, we often made our own entertainment. We arranged ourselves on the old sofas and chairs in this comfortable room. Soon, from the hallway we heard high-pitched shrieking and wild laughing, and in walked four of the male students, dressed in outlandish female outfits, obviously culled from the grab bag. Complete with padded bras, they were impersonating women, doing a can-can dance, and acting stupid.

Suddenly, I couldn't breathe. I felt crushed and humiliated. If simply dressing like women got laughs, what did that say about me and the other actual women? No one else seemed upset, which made me feel even worse. I wanted to cry and scream. Instead, I jumped up and ran out of the chalet, down the path, until I had come to my favorite "thinking" bench overlooking a deep valley. I felt like I had been kicked in the stomach.

Just then Birdie, an older woman, British, and the only trained counselor on the staff, walked by. She saw me crying, sat down, and listened. Then she urged me to go back and tell them how I felt. Female impersonation, she said, was not respectful of God's creation and might even hide deeper problems. When I returned, I found everyone deep into a serious conversation about what had happened. After apologies and explanations—the old story about how this was just fun and not to take it personally—a date was set for a study of gender in the Bible, and this topic became included in the curriculum.

The next day I discovered a copy of Simone de Beauvoir's *The Second Sex* in the grab bag as I was hunting around. I read it voraciously and it seemed to confirm what I had been feeling. The stereotyped feminine role couldn't possibly be God's plan. In spite of the biblical passages they quoted at L'Abri about woman's place, to me the Bible did not say that women were inferior or subordinate to men. But, with my almost non-existent biblical and theological knowledge, I had no success trying to explain my ideas to these leaders, many of whom had gone to seminary or, at least, Bible college.

Needing to Study

One day, I was assigned to work at Birdie's house. She agreed with me that women should be able to work outdoors, and so she allowed me to work in her strawberry patch. Not that I was of much use in a garden, despite all my politically motivated desire to be assigned to one. Between my overzealous weeding, which took out as many strawberry plants as weeds, and my overzealous eating of the strawberries (Birdie also agreed that we didn't get enough fresh fruit here), I may have done more harm than good. But what did I know from gardening? I was just a girl from Newark.

There was a student from Canada also assigned to Birdie's garden. He showed me a paper he had brought with him from a small Christian graduate college in Vancouver, British Columbia, called Regent. The author, a woman student there, had written a biblical exegesis paper. She gave sound theological reasons why women's oppression was wrong, that it was not a command of God, but a result of human sin. I was astounded and strengthened. I reasoned that if Regent was a Christian school, and they had "let" her write a paper like that, then the interpretation I was getting at L'Abri was not the only possible one. Suddenly, I desperately wanted to go to that school. Maybe there I could learn Greek and Hebrew and re-translate the passages that bothered me. Maybe the well-meaning people here had just gotten hold of an inferior translation. Yeah, that was it. Maybe the problem was fixable.

When I discussed my desires with the leaders, they were kindly but skeptical. While it was fine to study the Bible, they said, I should realize that no matter what degrees I earned, as a Christian woman I could only teach females and children. I could never hold teaching authority over males. Naturally, they didn't believe in the ordination of women. That went without saying. And what was this school, anyway? They had heard of it and feared it was "liberal." I was such a young Christian, they said. If I had to go to school, I should stick to the ones they approved of, like Dallas Seminary.

But I was sure Regent was the place for me. Since everyone at L'Abri loved Birdie for her wisdom and discernment, I asked for her advice. Out of all the leaders, she alone encouraged me: "What are you waiting for?" she asked in her crisp British way. "No one is preventing you from going there. Send for the application." I did and felt exultant. But with so much negative opinion from others, I could only hope I was doing the right thing.

Before I made any other plans, though, the leaders insisted that I be baptized, as an external sign of my new birth. "But I already was baptized when I was eight," I protested. They insisted I didn't know what I was doing then, but I remained skeptical, so they sent me to see Dr. Schaeffer.

He agreed with them, saying, "No, that other baptism doesn't count. It was done by a priest. He couldn't have been a believer. It's best if you let me do it here. You need to make public what you have accepted in private."

"All right, what could it hurt?" I thought. Yet to me this second baptism seemed entirely unnecessary. My friends there, on the other hand, thought I was really fortunate to be baptized by Francis Schaeffer. On the day of the baptism I was given a lot of praise, attention, and even gifts by the leaders and students. I appreciated their well-meaning intentions, but inside I felt unmoved. This act did not cause a visceral change in me the way my first baptism had.

I only realized later that an insight was growing, born of my mixed-faith background and first-hand experience of religious and ethnic prejudice. This revelation had its roots in the Bible: that there should only be "one Lord, one faith, one baptism," and that Christianity was terribly fractured by believers not trusting one another's fidelity. Once again, my instincts had proven to be strong, and yet I still had trouble trusting them. I respected the leaders' knowledge; I did not question their sincerity, and they seemed to have my best interests at heart. Yet their expertise was often wielded to direct me down paths that I just somehow *knew* were not where God was leading me. More than ever, I realized I needed more education to back up my strong if inadequately expressed beliefs.

Supervising Chambermaids

My money was all gone, but I had several months to go before my airplane ticket expired and I would have to return to the States. After nearly eight months at L'Abri, I was ready to do something else. But if I left the community, I would have to earn money to support myself. Someone told me about a Christian-owned hotel in Château-d'Oex several hours away. I hitched there, and, since I knew French, I was hired as *ménagère*—or supervisor of the chambermaids. My mother would get a real kick out of this, I thought. She had always hated to clean and when she couldn't force me to do it, had always hired it out. I had little idea about the fine points of housecleaning.

The hotel owners, who were British, recruited their workers from various U.S. colleges, looking for Christian young people to serve as the hotel's chambermaids, waiters, and busboys. They said it was hard to find enough Swiss to do the work. During my stay, the students came from Baylor University in Texas. The young people felt it was an opportunity in Christian service and a way to get to Europe. Meals and rooms were provided, along with a small stipend.

The hotel served a Swiss clientele, notoriously particular about good housekeeping. The owner's wife showed me how to make beds perfectly, clean sinks perfectly, and make sure everything was up to their perfect standards. Since I was a supervisor, she said, my privilege was to have my own room, while the others doubled up. I was admonished to enforce high standards and good discipline.

I enjoyed my new chambermaid staff and we got along well immediately. Soon I was bringing them the leftover croissants at break and making sure they had the supplies they needed. We laughed a lot, and when necessary, I would clean right alongside them, although that was not part of the job description. On our off-time, we prayed together, had Bible studies, went skating, and became good friends.

I was at the hotel over the holidays. This would be the first time I celebrated Christmas away from home. Christmas had always been very uncomfortable back in New Jersey. Our bakery was packed with customers, the adults worked constantly, and my mother was disgruntled by having to give so much of her time to a Christian event. We had a tree upstairs in our apartment—I always begged for one—but the decorating was usually left to me. At night, during the season, I would furtively listen to Christmas carols, played low on my clock radio in the bedroom. On Christmas Eve, my brother and I would watch *"A Christmas Carol"* on television while the adults worked. On Christmas morning the two of us would watch each other open presents before we went down to help in the store. Always—behind the superficial happiness I tried to exhibit—was a sad longing I couldn't understand.

This time it would be different. After the hotel cleaning was done on Christmas Eve, I traveled back to the special church that L'Abri used every year for their special service. In the dimly lit chapel, I realized I was happy and completely unconflicted about this holiday for the first time. Finally, I thought, I was having a real Christmas.

I also had a future, for I had applied to, and been accepted by, Regent College. My plan was to work at the hotel until shortly before my ticket expired, return to the U.S. for a short visit at home, and then begin graduate studies in Vancouver. Although I intended ultimately to return to journalism, first, I had some intellectual problems with my newfound faith that had to be solved.

But one day, shortly after Christmas, an older British woman was assigned to my chambermaid staff. She seemed quite curious about every aspect of the business and spent long hours talking with me about the hotel. After a week, the owners called me in to their office and told me that I was being "let go" and this woman was replacing me. Although I had learned how to clean passably well, they said, I was not particular enough. As an example, the owner's wife took me to a room and stuck her finger deep down into the overflow drain on the back of the sink. Her finger came back with some grey sludge on it. Obviously, she said, this would not do.

What was worse, according to her, was that I was too friendly with my staff. I had no sense of hierarchy and did not know how to keep my place as a supervisor. When I asked who I was supposed to socialize, pray, and eat with, they said, "people on your own level." That left the maitre d' of the dining room and the head maintenance man.

I could see there would be no point in saying anything else. I just packed up, said my good-byes and left.

On the train, I felt confused and devastated. *"Wasn't this a Christian hotel? Weren't we all brothers and sisters? Shouldn't they have given me a chance to understand the situation, rather than quietly planting my replacement without my knowledge?"* I couldn't stop thinking about it. This was the only time I had ever been fired or even censured on a job. It was embarrassing but I had no choice but to return to L'Abri. When I arrived, people seemed really happy to see me. "Welcome home. We've missed you so much," they said at Beau Site. "Isn't it wonderful to see her face again?" I relaxed, resumed my studies, and was happy I didn't have to clean rooms anymore. It *did* feel like home and family here. How was I going to make it back in the U.S. without this community?

Going Back

I had learned how to live at L'Abri. Life, for the first time, seemed balanced, not hectic or stressful. It was so beautiful, so peaceful, and I felt very accepted. People cared about each other and I had made many close friends. Relationships mattered, not status, money, or things. I felt like a new person with a new life. Even my serious disagreement with the others over gender issues could not diminish the depth of my experience. Here I had been taken seriously, perhaps for the first time. They had tried to answer my many questions and they had sheltered me, giving me the time, space, and peace in order to sort out what really mattered. Also for the first time in my life, I did not feel an undercurrent of fear; I did not feel driven. These people had shown me how to know God better, how to study the Bible, how to pray, how to identify and debate theological questions. Both my heart and my mind now rested in God and I did not want to lose that.

When I returned, there would be nowhere else to go but Newark and my parents' apartment. This would be difficult, especially because my parents were now convinced that I had joined a cult. At the time, the irony of a cult composed of conservative Presbyterians was lost on me. I had written to my parents about my spiritual discoveries, and got an angry letter back from my mother saying Jesus was *not* the Messiah and she would remain as she had always been, a Jew. My father appended a note saying I should do whatever made me happy, but I should certainly come home soon. What could I do in Newark? Should I "witness" to them further, as I was taught was my responsibility as a Christian? What should I say to my journalist friends? And what about my feminist friends? Or should I just keep a low profile until it was time for me to leave for school?

Chapter Seven

Another Kind of Shelter

I arrived at New York's JFK Airport, cleared customs, and put on my very heavy backpack, which nearly bent me double. I was apprehensive about being there, afraid of resuming my pre-conversion life. No one would understand how changed I felt, but I had already been gone a year, and it was time to return. My parents were there to pick me up.

"My God, what are you carrying?" my father said, as he rushed over.

"Dad, I've been doing this for a whole year. It's fine."

What he did not notice, however, were the two people following close behind me. I had been so worried about returning that Karen and Paul, two friends from L'Abri, had offered to come with me to Newark. My parents looked startled as I introduced them and said they'd be staying with us a few days. When I saw my parents' dismay, I felt even more anxious—but I was not surprised. I knew my mother and father were unused to overnight guests and even more unused to Protestants. Now, of course, I was a Protestant, too. After loading the car, we drove to Newark in near silence.

We arrived at Bloomfield Avenue, parked in front of the bakery, and brought the luggage upstairs to my parents' apartment. Then the five of us settled ourselves in the living room. Karen and Paul flanked me on the sofa like bodyguards. Cars and trucks whizzed outside as we tried to make some strained small talk about our flight. Finally my mother went to the kitchen to make dinner. My father turned on the television, my friends stayed on the couch, and I went into my bedroom to unpack. I cranked up my stereo really loud, playing music I used to enjoy before I went away. I knew it was wrong to block everyone out, but I just couldn't seem to help it.

My parents were convinced that I had joined a cult. It hadn't helped that I had brought along Karen and Paul, who must have looked like a couple of protectors sent from cult headquarters. While I empathized with my parents' discomfort, I was also dismayed that they could so misunderstand what I had done. What, I wondered, could be more mainstream than becoming a Protestant?

My friends stayed six days, long enough to help me find a church. L'Abri counseled people going back into "the world" that the most important thing was to find a "Bible-believing" church. But I had no idea how to do this. Despite my year among evangelicals, I found the larger world of Protestantism almost as alien as did my parents. For one thing, there were so many denominations. And how could I distinguish between those Christians who were "liberal" and those who were "really" Christian, as I had been instructed? It would've been easier to find a Catholic church—they each had a very similar liturgy, and you just went to the one in your parish. But, after my indoctrination at L'Abri—that would not do anymore.

We looked in the phone book and chose a Baptist one nearby that had "Bible-believing" in large letters in its ad. The service seemed fine that first Sunday, but after I attended on my own for several weeks, I realized it was not a good fit. Not only was it more conservative than L'Abri— here women did not even speak in church, much less teach or preach—but shortly after I began attending, the pastor told me that, if I wanted to join, I would have to be re-baptized—again! He said my previous two baptisms were just "sprinklings" rather than complete immersions, so they didn't count. By now, even *I* knew that yet another baptism couldn't be right.

Meanwhile, I had gotten used to being in community, and I missed it very much. The last vestige of L'Abri—Karen and Paul—had moved on to California. My first attempt to find a church community had not worked out, and—worst of all—my family felt almost like strangers to me. One day, riding in the backseat of my parents' car, I took a chance and enthusiastically related to my mother how I now considered myself a "completed Jew." I thought this would please her since I was claiming my Jewish heritage. Instead she became extremely angry, not even turning around as she said: "I already told you, Jesus is *not* the Messiah. I don't want to hear any of this ever again."

The first time I visited the Jewish side of the family after my return home, my Uncle Buddy expressed concern that I had joined "Jews for Jesus." Aunt Roslyn and her husband were very involved in the New York Jewish community, known and respected. Everyone loved Uncle Buddy, a decorated war veteran, as well as a good storyteller, humorous, and fun-loving. After World War II, he had dedicated himself to serving the needs of Jewish servicemen, becoming the New York State Commander of the Jewish War Veterans. The walls in their Bronx apartment were covered with awards, plaques, and commendations. But though he was an open-minded New Yorker, he condemned "Jews for Jesus" for proselytizing people born Jewish, thus further decimating Jewish ranks.

"No, really, Uncle Buddy," I protested, "that's not the group I joined. I just went from being a Catholic to a Protestant. No big deal," I apologetically explained. Looking a little dubious, he nevertheless said: "Okay, fine—as long as you'll still

eat chopped liver, I'll still love you" and then changed the
subject. Back again rushed that longing I had always felt.
I thought my conversion would change that, but it didn't.
While I knew I still was part of the *mishpocheh,* the whole big
family, I felt troubled that, by following my heart, in effect I
was being disloyal to them.

As for my Catholic relatives, they seemed worried that I
had somehow become less Italian now that I was a Protestant.
They figured that Italians were Catholics, and that was
that—so what if they didn't go to church very often. And
besides, Protestants had boring food and no culture. "Linda,
what now, you're not going to eat *scungilli* anymore?" teased a
cousin's husband. Again, I felt disloyal.

Next, I wanted to share my joy with my old journalism
friends. To be perfectly honest, I also thought they were
going to hell and needed me to tell them the good news of
the gospel. So I spent several days going around visiting
them and "witnessing" about my newfound faith. I was surprised at their universally negative reactions—to my faith
in general and to my new professional plans in particular.
How could I have turned down the job offer from *The Bergen
Record* (which I had done by letter from Switzerland), they
asked, and chosen instead to study the Bible in Canada? If
they had written a newspaper article about me, the head-
line would have read: "Feminist Turns Fundamentalist." Now
I didn't feel comfortable with anyone anymore. While my
conversion had made *me* feel whole, it seemed to be separat-
ing me even further from others.

Everything Good

After a month with my parents, it was time to leave for
school. I needed a cheap way to get out to Vancouver (since
I had sold my old Saab sedan to get money for tuition and

living expenses). So I bought an Ameripass, which for a flat fee allowed me a month of unlimited travel on Greyhound buses throughout North America. I planned to zigzag my way across the continent to Vancouver, visiting all those friends I had made at L'Abri. Most of them were new converts, too, and had gone back to "unbelieving" friends and family in the U.S. I wanted to see how my faith family—now separated and living in "pagan" outposts around the country—was doing.

On a beautiful spring day, my father dropped me off at the bus station in downtown Newark. He had been trying to dissuade me from traveling this way for weeks. As usual, he kept upping the ante to get me to change my mind: "I'll pay for your airfare and ship your things for you, if you don't do this," he said desperately. But I had the inexperienced optimism of a twenty-six-year-old, plus confidence from my year in Europe.

"Come on, Daddy, we've already discussed this. It will be perfectly safe. I'll be staying with friends on each stop. I'll call you every day, okay?" My planned stops were in Ohio, Colorado, Arizona, California, and Washington. While traveling in between, I read all the books Regent College suggested as preparation for my degree program. The reading oriented me to biblical studies and the history and theology of Protestantism. While it had a tone familiar to me from L'Abri—namely that evangelicals were the "true Christians"— it was not quite as world-denying or conservative as L'Abri, and that was a relief. Instead, it had a hopeful tone, suggesting that a committed faithful minority could have a positive effect on society. Between this study and my invigorating visits with friends, I arrived in Vancouver feeling happier than I had ever been in my life.

Although the L'Abri people had claimed Regent was "liberal," in fact it was quite evangelical. Founded in 1968 as a "transdenominational" school for serious lay education, it was located on the beautiful campus of the University of British Columbia. It was better for me that Regent was not a seminary. At a conservative seminary, I would have felt second-class since, at this time, most evangelicals did not believe in the ordination of women. Of course, ordination had not yet crossed my mind. Nothing in my background led me to believe this would be possible. Regent was a good fit for me—it was informal, intellectual, and sociable. The faculty was very accessible and students came from many different professional fields and religious backgrounds, all taking time out to explore their faith.

Eager to begin, I arrived in Vancouver a month before the fall semester started. The school helped me find a room in a cute little rented house with two other female students. It seemed miraculous that one of these women, Gail, was the very student whose paper had brought me here. Now that I was a Christian, everything seemed to be working out perfectly. Maybe I'd even meet a great Christian guy here, get married and have a family. I would finally have a one-faith home, my kids would know who they were, and we would go to church together.

Perfectly Surprised

I also arrived early so I could take the three-week intensive Greek course. My personal agenda required that I be able to do serious biblical exegesis right away. If I were going to solve the puzzle of well-meaning Christians using the Bible to subordinate women, I needed to know what the relevant passages said in the original languages. But the pace of the Greek course was relentless, requiring more self-discipline than I had exercised in years. Soon I was doing nothing but studying Greek, sleeping, and eating. Finally, it was the end of the third week. Now I planned to spend the entire weekend cramming so I would be ready for the exam on Monday. Once the final class ended, I gathered up my books and left the classroom. In the hallway, I paused to gaze out a window at the downpour, trying to adjust myself to this constant feature of life in rainy Vancouver. "Well," I thought, "at least I won't be distracted by good weather."

Suddenly, I felt a tap on my shoulder. I turned around to see—of all people—Jeff from *The Daily Record*. This was the guy who had both attracted me and scared me. This was the guy I had left the country to avoid. When I saw him, a shock went through my entire body, and my back muscles spasmed as though someone had slammed me from behind with a two-by-four. He stood there grinning with satisfaction. "I *knew* I'd find you," he said.

At first I was angry and a bit fearful. All my new hopes suddenly felt in jeopardy. As I stood there rooted to the ground and shaking, he told me his story. When I left the paper, he said, he had been upset and quit, too. After a year of bumming around, he learned from mutual friends that I had gone to Canada. Since he was determined to have his say, he used his reporter skills to track me down. A year ago, I would have argued with him, but I was different now and, as I listened, my feelings changed from anger to wonder. The evangelicals had taught me to interpret everything from a spiritual perspective. So, I thought, maybe God was involved in all of this. Maybe there was a purpose in it. Nevertheless, I realized suddenly that I still had to take the exam. I told Jeff I couldn't talk anymore but had to study. He agreed to spend the weekend touring and come back after I had taken the test.

Monday—right after the exam—Jeff appeared at my front door. We spent the next two days in conversation. I told him excitedly about my newfound faith—he kept insisting I would "get over it." He said he had found his own kind of peace in nature. In addition, he repeated, as he always had, that we were meant for each other and that I would eventually marry him. I vehemently disagreed, saying that now things were different between us. I would only consider becoming involved with a Christian guy. Although I remained resolute on the surface, I could not lie to myself. I had to admit I was still attracted to him. I don't know if Jeff sensed this, but finally he realized he wasn't going to change my mind any time soon, so he left.

School began, and I was caught up in demanding course work and satisfying fellowship with my new friends. Nevertheless, I could not get Jeff out of my mind. I prayed constantly about it and began discussing my feelings with friends and teachers. Everyone said there must be a higher purpose and agreed to pray that Jeff would turn to God. Finally after several months, I was able to relax and leave the matter in God's hands.

Toward the end of the first semester, I returned from school to find Jeff's backpack and a note on my front porch. He said he wanted to see me and was in a nearby restaurant having coffee. I went into the house and anxiously paced around, alternately elated and concerned. When he appeared at my door a half hour later, he said: "Last time you told me something about God and I want to hear it again." "So . . . God was at work, after all," I thought jubilantly. But I was not completely surprised. After all, hadn't I been seeing miracles for over a year now?

I invited him in and for hours excitedly repeated what I had said about God, love, peace, and all that. When I exhausted myself and stopped, Jeff said he wanted to go to church. I thought about this for a second and then said, "But it's Monday. Where can we find a church service?" Then I remembered that Regent had its weekly chapel Tuesday mornings. "Oh, I know," I said. "You can stay here in our back room and then come to chapel with me tomorrow."

The next day we attended the Regent chapel. Afterwards, I enthusiastically introduced him to the friends and professors who had been praying for him. Everyone seemed pleased but almost matter-of-fact, as though they had expected this all along. Then Dr. Houston, the president, invited Jeff to meet with him in his office while I went to class. When they emerged an hour later, Jeff quickly walked away. Before I could follow him, the president took my arm and said: "Let him go off by himself now for a while. Your friend has just accepted Christ."

I was grateful, exultant, and joyful. This was obviously all part of some larger plan. And, I reasoned with relief, now that Jeff was a Christian, he would get over his problems, and we would live happily ever after. God was giving me a soul-mate, a Christian husband, and everything else I ever needed. That evening, we got engaged. It amazed me that Jeff had been right all along—we were meant for each other. The whole thing had been inevitable. My package was complete—I had faith, a community, important work to do, and now a fiancé. Jeff seemed to love me more than anyone ever had. I admitted I loved him and soaked up the attention. God was giving us the desires of our hearts.

Jeff moved to Vancouver, enrolled at Regent for the second semester, and moved into the men's dormitory. I passed that spring in a reverie, studying, seeing Jeff, and being with our friends. I expected that after graduation we would go into some form of Christian service and work side-by-side as we had done at the newspaper. I loved relating our story to people—meeting at the newspaper, going our separate ways, finding each other, finding faith. When spring break came, we decided to visit our former newspaper buddy, Joyce, who now lived in northern California. Joyce had constituted one of my "signs from God" when she wrote me, shortly after my conversion in Switzerland, that she too had become a Christian. When she heard about Jeff's conversion, she had been overjoyed and begged us to visit her.

Unfortunately, we had no car, no income, and no expendable funds for travel. But a good friend of ours owned an old hippie van. His truck was purple, with bunk beds in the back and plenty of seating. One day he announced that he was taking a trip back to see his parents in California. He had to go right through Joyce's town, and he knew we wanted to see our friend, so he invited us and a few other students along. In the pictures we took before leaving, we are a motley group—five men and one woman, all wearing our ragged jeans and flannel shirts, standing in front of a purple converted bread truck with flowers painted on it.

We must have looked like a little group of drug-packing hippies, because as we approached the U.S.-Canadian border at Blaine, Washington, the border guards immediately pulled us over. "Let's put our Bible on the dash," said John, the driver. "They'll see we are Christians and maybe won't make things difficult for us." But his strategy didn't help a bit. The guards looked very suspicious and made us get out while they searched the vehicle from top to bottom. Still not satisfied, they lined us up and asked each of us where we were born. "Menominee, Michigan," said Jeff. "Los Angeles," said John. "New York," said another. When it was my turn, the guards still looked leery. "Okay, where were you born?" they asked belligerently, perhaps hoping that I, the lone woman, would slip up and reveal something. "Newark, New Jersey," I said. The guard looked surprised, paused, and then said with a laugh. "Okay, you can go. *Nobody* would make *that* up." He smiled and waved us through.

Our visit with Joyce was glorious, as we all reveled in

the amazing work of God, converting us from secular, cynical journalists to committed Christians with meaning and purpose in our lives. We told Joyce that—although we had moved a long way from our former lives in New Jersey—our wedding would be held back there that summer. My parents wouldn't consider anything else. They had met Jeff already, were pleased that I was getting married, and wanted to help us to do it right. Even so, I still felt bad about my previous short-lived marital mistake, and did not want to make my parents pay for a second wedding. I had learned from being in community that lots of money wasn't necessary to hold a special event. So Jeff and I decided that, rather than renting a hall, we would have a simple outdoor wedding in a friend's backyard. My parents balked, but finally accepted it.

However, my mother drew the line when I suggested that it could be—like all our Regent parties—potluck. "What . . . I should ask Aunt Louise to bring a casserole? Are you kidding? Do you want me to die?" she said with true horror. So my parents hired a caterer and made our wedding cake. Everyone from all our various life stages was invited. Jeff and I agreed that it was the happiest day of our lives. This, surely, was what heaven would be like—a big party. We even had a jeweler in Philadelphia make up identical wedding rings, from a mold designed by an artist friend of ours. The thick gold rings had three panels with symbols representing our special story. On the inside was engraved "Delight yourself in the Lord and He will give you the desires of your heart."

Jeff's entire family flew in from various places in the Midwest. His was a large and very devout Catholic family. By marrying him, I gained a mother- and father-in-law who were proud of what I was doing, and six great sisters-in-law. Although they probably wished we were Catholic instead of Protestant, his mother confided in me that I had helped bring Jeff back to the faith, and that was enough for her. Someday, everyone expected, Jeff and I would add a child to their boisterous "family picnic" that was held in the same Michigan park every year. In the meantime, however, we would finish our educations. So, after a very brief honeymoon, we returned to Vancouver.

A Dual Life

Thus began what should have been a glorious life. But the truth turned out to be a lot more complicated.

My intellect blossomed as never before. I began the second year of my Master's degree with great enthusiasm, planning an ambitious thesis project that would help me determine whether the evangelical position on the role of women was right or wrong. My grades were good and I had lots of friends at school. In fact, Dori—the friend who had originally directed me to L'Abri—joined us in Vancouver that fall to begin a degree program. It was wonderful to have her there, and we marveled at how many things were coming together. Outwardly, Jeff and I were a successful young Christian couple. We threw great parties, shared domestic duties, and prided ourselves on having a truly liberated marriage, unlike many of our more conservative Christian friends.

But there was another story, too—a darker side to our personal lives. It began innocuously enough. One day before school was to start in the fall, Jeff announced that he would not be continuing at Regent. Instead, he said, he had decided to take a Master's degree in communications at nearby Simon Fraser University. This was my first inkling that maybe we would not have the bright future of Christian service together that I had hoped for. I was disappointed but reconciled myself to his decision, figuring that as long as he was doing what he liked, things would work out. He started well, but the longer he studied there, the more he became conflicted between the Christian community at Regent and the more Marxist orientation of his favorite professors, who decried religion as a crutch and sometimes an evil.

Soon our happy times together began to diminish. Although Jeff insisted he was still a Christian, he made me the brunt of his growing skepticism with religion. I often felt that Jeff was baiting me, but I didn't know how to avoid taking the bait. It seemed that every day, before I realized what was happening, we were involved in yet another argument. We fought about religion, about politics, about gender roles. We struggled over how to spend the little money we had since, on our student visas, we were not allowed to work and earn more. Our shouting got so loud that I worried about our neighbors, for we lived in the midst of a small community of Regent students.

In addition, Jeff's old unpredictability began to reassert itself. One minute he was practically worshiping the ground I walked on; and the next I could do nothing right. He would find fault with how I washed the dishes, what I wore, or how I talked with my friends. I learned to guard my opinions and feelings, based on his current mood. I hid in my schoolwork and intensified my prayer life. The peace I had found at L'Abri and thought I had found at Regent was quickly unraveling.

Things really fell apart my third year at Regent. One day early in the term, I came home to find Jeff fuming about a letter he was holding. His graduate department was offering him a student assistantship, complete with salary. This sort of work was permitted by the Canadian government since it was part of his education. I took the letter from him, read it, and said excitedly: "Wow, this is great! It's such an honor, Jeff. I knew they would recognize your potential. And the money will really be a help."

Jeff looked at me menacingly and said: "Well, you might

like academia and ass-kissing. That's how you are, all religious and holy. But I don't want to pander to them. I'm not going to do it. So what, if they pay me?" He added, in a taunting tone: "Why do you care about money? Where's your faith, if you're such a good Christian?" Then he turned his back on me and busied himself with something else. "I don't understand," I said, starting to cry. "Why is this bad? Why don't you want to take it? The teaching will be great experience and even fun." He acted like I wasn't there so, angry and frustrated, I poked the back of his leg with my foot to get his attention.

He swiveled around and there was rage in his face. In an instant, he knocked me to the floor and twisted my left arm backward. There was a loud crack, sharp pain, and I knew immediately it was broken. Jeff never stopped yelling. So, with his voice in my ears, I braced my arm tight against my body, went out of the house, and took a bus to Vancouver General Hospital. When they asked me how this had happened, I told them my husband had done it. Beyond that, I said very little as they encased my arm in a large, right-angled plaster cast from bicep to wrist. I was afraid to make a fuss or call attention to myself. It never even occurred to me to press charges. With both of us on student visas, I feared that Immigration would make us leave the country if the authorities got involved. So, in shock and not knowing where else to go, I returned home and actually slept in the same bed with Jeff that night.

The next day I got up very early and, in a daze, took a bus to campus, then wandered around where I wouldn't see anyone I knew. Eventually, I found myself talking to the university's Dean of Women. I'm not really sure how I ended up with her, but when she heard what had happened, she arranged for me to stay for several nights with an administrator of nearby Vancouver School of Theology, located on another side of campus. The administrator was exceptionally kind and gentle to me. She also happened to be a registered nurse, and as she fixed up a bedroom for me in her apartment, she said: "Just pretend you are my own daughter and let me take care of you. A broken arm is serious. Your body is in shock."

I was grateful to be there. I slept a lot, ate the meals she prepared for me, and finally felt safe. Even in my distraught condition, though, I noted that this Protestant woman did not know how to prepare spaghetti, using a puree of vegetables on top, instead of tomato "gravy." Oh well, I thought, I guess food isn't everything. In fact, being with this kind woman felt almost like being with God—protected, safe, accepted, and loved. And this was an administrator of a seminary I had been warned was "too liberal." Several days later, after the two women administrators conferred, they sent me to a domestic violence shelter on the outskirts of town.

Another Kind of Shelter

"L'Abri" means "The Shelter," but my shelter in Vancouver was entirely different from the one I enjoyed in Switzerland. This shelter was in a nondescript little house in a run-down suburban neighborhood about ten miles from the city. Its location was kept a secret, and we were admonished to stay inside in case some prowling, violence-prone husband or boyfriend should be looking for us. I felt as if I were in prison and, although I was exhausted, I couldn't relax. Instead, my mind went round and round: "*How did I end up here? This isn't supposed to happen. I'm a feminist. He's a feminist. He's a pacifist. We're both educated. We're Christian.*"

When I explained all this to the counselor conducting my intake interview at the shelter, she rolled her eyes. "Obviously he *isn't* any of those things," she said. "And if you go back to him, as many of the women do, you'll eventually end up dead. We've seen it over and over again." With one gesture and one speech, she shattered my identity. *I* was supposed to be the feminist and the helper, not the victim. *I* was supposed to be her, helping the less fortunate, the less educated, those mired in sexism. Instead, I was like all the other women here—hurt, angry, afraid. In fact, with the large cast on my arm, I looked worse than any of them.

"My dad's a big asshole," said one preteen girl to me in the fenced-in backyard one day. "Me and my mom will never go back." She looked too angry and bitter for a girl her age. The other children there, too, seemed hyperactive, nervous, and afraid. The staff tried to calm and play with them, but the place still felt like bedlam. A woman who looked about seventy roomed with me. She didn't say much but chain-smoked constantly, every now and then saying "shit" to no one in particular. How could I have gone from my nice, motivated evangelical community to this painful place? I was afraid to go back home but, maybe worse, ashamed to go back to school. I was sure they would think I had deserved the violence because of my strong views on women's rights.

After nearly a week there, all the time wearing the same clothes, I just left without saying anything and walked the whole way back to the city. I had no money, no bankbook, no credit card. Not knowing where to turn, I automatically found myself at my college and sat down on the grass in front of the building. The first person to spot me was Dori. She ran over to me, saying, "Where have you been? You've been missing for days! We were worried." I told her the whole story. At first she was speechless, but then she said, "I warned you about him when we worked at *The Daily Record*. I told you we went to the same college and he was weird there, too. But you wouldn't listen. You said he was your best friend."

Dori went inside to let the school administrators know what had happened. They took immediate action, arranging for me to stay with a church member until they could figure out what to do next. I was still dazed but grateful that they had taken over. I sensed no judgment or admonitions. No one, at least to my face, blamed my plight on my feminism. Later that day, the Dean and a church elder took me back to my apartment to get some things. I waited in the car while the elder hustled Jeff off for a walk. Then the Dean came with me inside and helped me throw a few clothes in a suitcase and my books in a small daypack. Back in the car, we waited while the elder brought Jeff back to our apartment. When the elder returned, he told us Jeff had been recalcitrant, unrepentant, angry, and blamed me for everything. Later a plan was set up to have several men of the church meet with Jeff every morning, buy him breakfast, pray, and talk.

Provincial social services also got involved, alerted by the doctor who had set my arm. They contacted me to offer psychotherapy. Before I agreed to therapy, I phoned the psychiatrist who taught some courses for Regent to ask his advice. I felt I could trust him, but rather than reassuring me as I had expected, he said, "Well, this is not a small thing. It's very serious. You might never be able to live with him again." Panicky, stunned, and distraught, I quickly ended the conversation. But I did sign up for therapy at the nearby provincial clinic. The therapist assigned to me was not impressed when I told her about our feminist marriage. She became especially negative when I related that we were hoping to start a family soon. "No, not now," she said. "This would definitely *not* be the time." I was devastated. All my dreams were being thrown off track, one after the other.

As for Jeff, I later learned that social services had contacted him to take their course for perpetrators of domestic violence. He attended a couple of sessions but refused to continue, insisting he was not like the "biker guys with their chains and boots." He was sure the abuser profile did not fit him. That pretty much ended his efforts to seek help. While

Jeff remained in our apartment, I spent weeks being hosted by various people from church and school. Finally, the Dean and his wife invited me to stay at their house as long as I needed. They encouraged me to continue with my degree and not to return to Jeff until I was sure that the violence would not recur. I stayed there for many weeks, but one day Jeff phoned me and said he had a "word from God" that this would never happen again. Against the advice of the Dean, I believed Jeff and returned home.

I had no way to sort all this out. I wanted to believe the episode was an aberration. There were no books on domestic violence that I knew of, certainly none from a Christian perspective. I was in the dark. When I returned to school, no one mentioned our situation, even though I attended class with the cast on my arm. In fact, many of my classmates avoided me or looked at me strangely. The elders at our church—which prided itself on never having a divorce among its members—encouraged us to join a "cell group" which provided weekly Bible studies, prayer, support, and the oversight of an elder and his wife. With their help, things seemed to settle down and our marriage seemed restored. At both school and church, most people assumed a "hands-off" attitude, acting as though the violence had never happened. No one, except the medical professionals, suggested that this was a crisis situation, horribly wrong, or that anything should be done.

Although Jeff and I continued to have arguments, they were more restrained. I put the violence out of my mind and forgave Jeff, as I had been taught a Christian was supposed to do. I still felt the need to tiptoe around him when his moods changed, but there were other things that seemed to be working well. I was proud of our shared domestic duties. I was grateful that he supported my desire to study. I felt very fortunate that we professed the same faith. These things were still major benefits, in my mind.

Good Theology

Not only that, but my research was going surprisingly well. I had come here to resolve my questions on "women's place," and even though hardly anyone at the school agreed with me, I was finding much evidence—historical, biblical, and theological—to prove that the subordination of women was sin, not salvation. For my Master's thesis, I examined how the church had interpreted one of the key Bible passages used to justify inequality: 1 Corinthians 11:2–16. I found that its interpretation had not only changed over the years, but was done in direct reaction to changes in the culture.

I was realizing that the subordination of women, just like slavery (which at one time had also been justified biblically), was not a command of God—as I had been taught—but an accommodation to or reaction against society. I was becoming convinced that liberation, not hierarchy, was the true import of the gospel, and of Jesus' life and death. The longer I studied, prayed, and pondered it all, the stronger my beliefs became. In the end, I titled my thesis "From Hierarchy to Equality."

I also became able to explain why the conservative stand against the ordination of women was misguided. I had begun getting opportunities—through the burgeoning new movement known as "Christian feminism"—to lead seminars and publish articles. People told me I was good at this and I wanted to do more of it. Yet, if my vocation was teaching and that helped people, wasn't that a ministry? And if I, as a woman, could minister in this way, why couldn't I be ordained to do it? All I knew was that I had always felt drawn to the church, loved studying theology, and felt this was the most vital, energizing work I had ever done.

Yet whenever I spoke about my research, many fellow students seemed skeptical of my findings, especially the men who thought my feminist leanings made me a radical. Although I was growing more confident of my convictions, I did not particularly like being characterized this way. Every time I'd talk with them, hear a lecture, or read something sanctioning the subordination of women, I'd rush to the same stall in the basement women's lavatory and start crying. Then I would pray: "*If this is true, God, help me believe it. And if it isn't, give me some answers.*" Invariably, I'd go back to the library, study more, and find some new insight that gave me hope. At this time, I only dimly perceived that my marital life graphically illustrated the clash of male dominance and female strivings for equality. I doubt that Jeff realized this either. But later this gender clash, especially the violence, would fuel my passion for teaching and my motto: "Bad theology kills."

When my Master's thesis was finished, I asked the faculty if I could have an "oral defense." In this standard academic model, usually used for doctoral dissertations, faculty members question the scholar about their findings, looking for loopholes or faulty design. Several professors had become enthusiastic about my topic, so they set up the debate. That spring day our small library was "standing-room-only" for the event. I don't know if the crowd was expecting an indictment or a vindication.

The debate went well and at the end the faculty gave my thesis their open approval. Suddenly I was popular, and people were asking to read my work. So, with Professor Ward Gasque's help, my thesis was published as a book. The day it arrived I sold the entire initial print run of 500 copies right out of the box in the college coffee room. Soon I was reprinting it to meet demand. It amazed me how quickly opinion could change. One day I was a heretic, the next a hero.

But graduation loomed ahead, and I still wasn't sure what I would do with my degree. The president of the college suggested that after graduation I become his secretary and help edit his writing. This didn't seem right, but I had no female role models to give me an idea of what else was possible. My life had changed dramatically and, as much as I had enjoyed journalism, I felt called to something else now. Among my class, many of the male students were planning to pursue Ph.D.s to teach theology or biblical studies, and some were deciding to become pastors. When I heard them discussing such plans, I felt a strong yearning. Why couldn't I do these things, too?

Jeff supported my desire for an advanced degree. When I discussed this at school, at first the professors tried to discourage me, but eventually a few began to support the idea. While they didn't believe women should be ordained, they had fewer problems with women teaching. Perhaps, they said, once I got a Ph.D., I would be able to find a job in a Christian college or seminary. I assumed that was what I would do and felt fortunate. I had gotten used to the evangelical world. Small and close-knit, it was almost a culture unto itself. In fact, it was kind of like my Italian and Jewish background but with blander food and more restrained emotions. I had made lots of friends, knew many of the scholars in this world, and felt I could work alongside of them. I was married to a Christian, expected to have a family, and was active in a local church. I fit in as well here as I had anywhere.

However, niggling doubts kept me from wholeheartedly embracing this plan. For I knew implicitly that even if I *could* get a job in an evangelical institution—and there were very few women professors at such schools then—I'd be under more intense scrutiny and expected to play a more circumscribed role. My hard questions would scare people, yet I knew I could not stop asking them.

If the evangelical world offered me few options, then what about pursuing education and employment opportunities in the larger, liberal mainstream? Although my adult Christian practice had been formed within a tradition that considered liberalism a threat, even an enemy, all along my intuition had suggested otherwise. And eventually my education had offered me enough confidence and, more important, biblical evidence to argue that labels like "liberal" and "radical" were as fractious and demeaning to the Christian community as re-baptisms or the subordination of women: "in Christ there is no Jew or Greek, slave or free, male or female"; "one faith, one baptism."

Recent, dramatic experience supplied me with additional evidence of the sinfulness of labels. Although I had received considerable support from my church and school community during the marital crisis, I had also received grace through the university Dean of Women, and through the administrator of the "liberal" seminary down the road. As a result, I began spending more time at VST, especially when I learned they had a women's center. It seemed amazing that they had a room, books, and a staff all devoted to probing women's issues in the church. As I got to know them, I felt concerned that many at my college dismissed these people. I wondered if the problem was simply that they didn't know each other well enough. If we interacted more, I thought, we would see our unity as Christians. But when I enthusiastically suggested to the center's director that the two schools could form a joint women's coalition, she looked down, shook her head and said sadly, "No, Linda, they won't go for it. They think we are just liberals and not really Christian." Her hopeless tone really struck me.

I finished out the year and graduated. We spent an additional year in Vancouver while Jeff worked on his degree. I spent the time helping edit *Crux*, the school's journal, and learning Hebrew—something I had always wanted to do. I got more comfortable with the idea of doing a Ph.D., so I began preparing for the Graduate Record Exam and brushing up my French. Jeff and I discussed where I might apply. We agreed I would be better off at a more mainstream institution where my study and career goals would be less hampered. I could maintain my faith there, I was sure, and yet have intellectual freedom and more acceptance as a woman.

We selected locations that would work for both of us. Jeff favored Princeton but I wasn't sure I wanted to move back to New Jersey. I favored the University of Chicago Divinity School, but Jeff didn't want to live that near his family. Finally, I applied to Yale, Vanderbilt, Princeton Theological Seminary, Iowa, and the Graduate Theological Union in Berkeley. Although Princeton gave me the best offer, and I received acceptances from all the other schools, Jeff and I decided that radical Berkeley was a good choice. My dream had always been to go to graduate school there. As for Jeff, northern California was close enough to Vancouver that he could drive back periodically as he finished his thesis. So, happily, we made plans to move to Berkeley.

Chapter Eight

Margins to Mainstream

We arrived in Berkeley, where I was to begin my doctoral studies at the Graduate Theological Union (GTU), located on the edge of the University of California campus. The school assigned us an old yet stylishly Art Deco apartment on Le Conte Avenue, with a beautiful view of the Bay. The first night there we discovered it was infested with quite fearless German cockroaches. Neither lights nor sprays nor waving hands scared them away. Until the maintenance department could send over an exterminator, we stored our plates and foodstuff in the refrigerator, and worried all night that they would crawl into bed with us. Not an auspicious beginning, but it would take more than cockroaches to dampen our enthusiasm at being in this exciting new environment.

Berkeley made Vancouver look downright sedate. Jeff and I went frequently to the many coffee shops, bookstores, and ethnic restaurants in order to revel in the open-minded environment. The first thing we noticed were the street people. Clearly many were mentally ill, but they were mostly tolerated. The "Woo Man" stood in the same place every day, repeating "woo" over and over. The "Polka Dot Man" was consistently dressed in clothes painted with large dots. A shabbily, but professorially, dressed man moved around on Shattuck Avenue repeating high-level mathematical formulas.

According to Jeff, even the seminary library had its own

resident character. Every time Jeff used the men's room, he noted a youngish man always dressed in the same uniform of white shirt and black pants, always carrying a tattered brown paper bag. It was filled with bars of Ivory soap, which the young man used for frequent, even obsessive scrub-downs—like a pre-op surgeon. While there was an odd suit-ability in this man's choice of a religious locale to act out his cleanliness obsession, Jeff was concerned that he needed help. When he mentioned the odd behavior to one of the library's staff, however, he was informed: "We don't bother anyone here. This is Berkeley."

Also very striking were the "after-eaters." In front of many downtown restaurants, shabbily dressed people peered into display windows, noting which tables were about to be va-cated. When the paying guests got up, the after-eaters would rush in to finish off the remains. Amazingly, the busboys and waiters rarely interfered but politely hung back until the after-eaters were finished. And tacked to every blank wall and pole were layers and layers of posters protesting, advertising, and defending all sorts of things; some we agreed with, such as nuclear disarmament, but others we could hardly believe were openly proclaimed, such as pederasty.

Jeff worked at odd jobs, while I found a student work-study job at GTU's Center for Women and Religion. Finally, I thought, I was in a place that allowed me to be as free as I wanted. I enthusiastically participated in their activities and one day bought a ticket for a Center fundraiser. To my surprise, I won a free, comprehensive checkup at the recently opened wom-en's health clinic on Market Street in San Francisco.

Good Theology

Jeff and I felt hip and radical as we traveled into San Francisco for the exam. *"This should be good,"* I thought. *"Everyone here is a feminist, and they will be really sensitive and thorough.*" I liked the idea of a full workup, but was confident everything would be fine. After the exam, the female physician came in to speak with me. She said she had discovered a fibroid tumor. While benign, such things usually presented a troublesome, although not life-threatening, gynecological problem.

As I absorbed this news, she busied herself with paperwork. Then she looked over at me and added matter-of-factly: "Well, you can easily solve the problem by having a hysterectomy." I was shocked speechless. Finally, I squeaked out, "But . . . but . . . I'm planning to start a family." I couldn't believe I was getting this advice in a women's clinic. Weren't they, of all people, supposed to care about preserving women's bodies?

I mumbled something about checking with my regular doctor, got dressed, and returned to Jeff in the waiting room. After I told him, we both left the clinic in a daze. We had been trying to have a child for several months now. We still remembered the benediction given three years previously by our Jewish goldsmith. When we had picked up our rings, thanking him for his efforts with the complicated design, this man beamed at us and said: "*Mazel Tov.* You are going to have beautiful children!"

Although my feminist consciousness-raising had made me afraid of the demands a child would bring, I had no desire to remain childless. Such a state was anathema to my Jewish roots and equally unacceptable to the Italian side. I had grown up with family all around me, enjoyed it, and couldn't imagine life any differently. "Having a child just makes life better," my father had said once with a lot of feeling. Jeff felt the same way. His family was much larger than mine and still growing. They were waiting for us to catch up.

Now, in addition to my doctoral studies and my work at the center, I began looking into this medical problem. My "free" medical exam initiated a round of tests, drugs, and medical interventions that would last for several years. Not only that, but this upsetting development added to a serious academic problem that had presented itself. I had discovered that the program at GTU was not really right for me. By now, I was planning to become a theologian and study the history of doctrine, for I wanted to understand how beliefs had changed over time. My GTU advisors said if I wanted to study doctrine prior to the Enlightenment period, I'd have to do it as a historian. But I wanted to be a theologian who knew the historical sweep of Christian doctrine.

So—blocked both personally and professionally—I began to rethink our move to Berkeley. Jeff was nearly finished with his Master's thesis and had not found a good job. He was open to my transferring somewhere else and, for the first time since my conversion experience, I began to think it might be better to live near family. So I phoned Princeton Theological Seminary, a Presbyterian school, where I had been accepted the year before.

In Berkeley, we had begun attending a Presbyterian church. Through them, I discovered that the denomination fit me well. It had a high concern for intellectual integrity, was theologically moderate, and had a clearly defined set of beliefs that connected with my earlier exposure to Reformed theology at L'Abri. Princeton Theological Seminary would be perfect. It was like the Vatican of Presbyterianism, had very credible Ph.D. programs, and also prepared people for ministry. History of doctrine was understood there as a theological pursuit. So I was elated when they eagerly agreed to re-accept me.

They also agreed that I could delay starting until winter, a helpful break that would allow me to spend some time focusing on the infertility issue—which had thrown me into not just a medical crisis, but a spiritual one as well. I couldn't understand how infertility could happen to me. Wasn't I doing all the right things? I had struggled to find faith, I had married another Christian, I was preparing to serve God by teaching, and, I had a completely normal desire to have a child. And what about my dream to have a one-faith family that would go to church together?

Like the domestic violence, infertility was a totally unexpected problem and I had no experience to draw upon. I and all the other young women I knew had been more concerned with preventing untimely pregnancy and with the oppressive patterns of sexism if we didn't play our "baby cards" just right. At the many women's groups I attended, we had intense conversations about how to combine career and family, talking for hours as though our very lives depended on it.

Now that I couldn't conceive, I felt abnormal, even cursed, as if the gods of sexism were somehow getting back at me for pursuing my career path. I once had laughed to read that Victorians believed if a woman used her brain too much, she risked sterility. They couldn't possibly be right, could they? No, that was ridiculous. Why had God given me a good mind if I wasn't supposed to use it? It didn't help when Jeff's family said regular novenas, gave me medals to pin on my underwear, and then, when they saw no results, began praying to St. Jude, the patron saint of hopeless causes. In spite of all this and reassurances by my doctor in Berkeley that things would work out, I wasn't getting pregnant. Maybe in New Jersey we would find a specialist who could help us have a child. And, in the meantime, it would be good to have the support of family nearby.

Route to Princeton

The semester off would also give me time to learn German. At Princeton, they acted as if German was the language of God. They required it of all Ph.D. candidates in theology.

Here was one language I had avoided, but now I had no choice. At first I tried studying German alone, and then with a tutor. Even though I made some progress in reading it, somehow I could not let the words come out of my mouth. I wondered if my mental block was somehow connected to my heritage: my Jewish side and my father's World War II service. My new interest in German certainly received no encouragement from my family.

"Why don't they make you learn Latin?" my father asked. "Now that's got to be important for religion. And Italian— shouldn't you be learning that? That's what they speak in Rome." Although I tried to explain the connection between German and Protestant theology, he remained puzzled. As the Jewish relatives would have said, my father "didn't know from Protestants."

He and my mother were even less enthusiastic about my final strategy to learn German. For I decided to spend the last month of my free semester—before starting doctoral studies at Princeton—in Germany, at the renowned language school, the Goethe Institute. I hoped that, if I went to Germany, some of my inherited prejudice would fade when I was face-to-face with real people. The complete immersion, plus lots of beer and wurst, would surely loosen my tongue.

Fortunately, I guessed right. The Goethe Institute worked for me—eventually. We had class every day, all day, but at first I remained silent, even though the goal was to practice as much as possible. The teacher had tried everything to get me to speak, and she and my classmates were getting frustrated. One day, our class got into a conversation about the Bible, the students all agreeing that it was thoroughly sexist and detrimental to women. After listening a while, I finally blurted out—in German—that they were wrong and I had found the gospel liberating. At this, the entire class applauded. After that—which looked suspiciously like an altruistic conspiracy to draw me out—I was fine. I finished the course, rejoined Jeff in New Jersey, and passed my language exam.

We rented a small apartment in Princeton's married students' housing, and the whole thing felt like a homecoming. For the first time, I was completely unconflicted about being in New Jersey. Jeff and I had met and married in New Jersey and still had friends here, including Dori. She had returned here after her one year at Regent. My relatives were also glad to have me back. They had all moved out of Newark but still lived relatively nearby. My life was finally coming together.

Even though New Jersey is a small state, the sociological distance between Newark and Princeton is about as far as you can get. My extended family was proud that I had made that journey. Of course, when my parents told their friends I was doing a Ph.D. at Princeton, they often left off the "Theological Seminary" part. Nor was my major, theology, highlighted in their conversation. All right, so maybe I didn't marry an Italian doctor or give them lots of children, but at least they could say I was going to Princeton.

Princeton was very different from Vancouver and Berkeley. For one thing, the people were all resolutely preppy in dress, a striking change after the hippy atmosphere at Berkeley. My wardrobe still consisted largely of jeans and colorful tops. One day Dori came to visit and wanted to see downtown Princeton. We drove there and walked into a clothing store on Nassau Street. It was a hot day, and we had on cutoff jeans. We both noted that it took forever to get someone to wait on us. The next week, to check out my perceptions, I went into the same store in a tan skirt and a navy blue blazer. I got waited on immediately. Okay, maybe it wasn't a scientific experiment, but it made an impression on me.

Princeton—both university and seminary—held a powerful symbolic and emotional sway over its community. Being at Princeton was a way many people formed their identity. New students at the seminary vied with each other to be identified as the smartest, the most worthy of this historic place. I was as impressed as anyone with the old buildings and beautiful campus. It seemed like a dream, being there. When I was in high school, Princeton didn't even take women, and I wouldn't have had the nerve to apply to an Ivy League school anyway.

But it was still heavily male-oriented. Frequently, I was the only woman in my theology classes. I felt I had to struggle to be taken as seriously as the male students. My comments often dropped like heavy stones in the middle of the seminar table, only to be taken up minutes later by some guy—and enthusiastically received. Not only that, but I found it hard to coldly criticize others' work, which put me at a serious disadvantage in the classroom, since developing this ability was an important part of the training.

At one point, I actually asked Jeff to teach me how to critique someone's work, since he was so good at it. I took his advice, and for the first time, received open praise from the professors. Rather than being pleased, I was dismayed. I felt like Goldie Hawn in the film *Private Benjamin*—the sheltered Jewish girl who enlists in the Army, tries to "make nice" rather than being a fierce competitor during basic training but doesn't win the approval of her fellow recruits until she finally erupts in anger during hand-to-hand combat training.

Welcome to Mainstream Protestantism

For the first three years at Princeton, I continued to have many medical tests and treatments, because we remained determined to have children. My parents were very supportive.

Finally I was doing something with which they could whole-heartedly agree. In fact, I amazed myself with the strength of my desire to have a child. Maybe I wasn't so weird after all. Yet, as is common for many who struggle with infertility, I felt ashamed that we were not successful at this most natural of acts. At school I didn't specifically identify the kind of medical problem I was having, or even talk about it too much. Such bodily matters were not common conversation in my department. But the emotional stress of the tests, surgeries, and cycles of hope and despair was hard to hide.

Eventually it spilled over to my work, prompting me to see certain theological issues in a new light. In one class on Karl Barth's Doctrine of the Trinity, I suggested that the three-in-one God creating out of love was similar to my husband and me wanting a child. We didn't *need* to have a child, I said, but it was a desire that flowed from our love. The professor didn't like my analogy. He thought I was saying God *had* to create, anathema in Christian theology. After class, several of the male students expressed amazement that I would actually *want* to get pregnant since it would obviously stall my career. Their comments almost made me feel dizzy. *They* all had spouses and families. Why I couldn't I want both, too? What was wrong with that?

Maybe they had a point, though, for I soon learned that the demands of the program didn't accommodate life crises too well. I had been awarded a teaching fellowship. But at the end of one semester, with many papers to grade, I unexpectedly found myself spending several nights in the hospital after a gynecological procedure. I had reacted badly to the anesthesia and was unable to sit up without getting sick. Flat on my back, I called my professor, explained the situation, and asked if he could give me a short delay on grading student papers. He sounded angry and questioned my devotion to the program, saying I was imposing on him and the others. I felt devastated by his reaction, but the responses of my fellow doctoral students weren't much better. I had told several of them that I would be in the Princeton hospital, just a few blocks from the seminary, but no one came to visit or inquired about me. They were probably too busy studying. That's how it was in my department: competitive and driven.

In fact, we often reacted guiltily when we saw each other out at a restaurant or other enjoyment. One day a fellow theology student walked into the Princetonian Diner, located right near married student housing. Jeff and I were having lunch with my parents, as we often did when they visited. "Oh, hi, Linda," the student said with a sheepish grin. "Why aren't you working on that huge Barth assignment? I have been reading that stuff since 6:00 a.m. and my wife wanted me to bring her a sandwich from here, so I figured I'd take a break," he said as he rushed over to the takeout counter. *"What kind of community is this, anyway?"* I wondered. They are refreshingly open-minded about theological issues, highly intelligent, and committed Christians. But why was work more important than each other? This unyielding Protestant ethos—cerebral, reserved, work-obsessed—was much more extreme here than what I had encountered among evangelicals.

Yet, in some important ways, Princeton provided what my ethnic background and the evangelical communities had lacked. Although the residual effects of sexism remained, here at least there was no theological dictum saying women were subordinate or limited in leadership potential. There were no ideological restraints on what I could do. The faculty fully expected me to find a job as a professor when I graduated. And, over time, I realized that my work was respected even though overt praise seemed to be anathema to these restrained Protestants.

Most important, the people I met at Princeton immediately recognized my vocation in ministry. No one had ever done this before, least of all me. During my first meeting with theology professor Dan Migliore, as we reviewed my study plans, he interjected, to my surprise: "Do you want to get ordained?" Never in my history with Catholics, Jews, alternative religions, or evangelical Protestants had I been asked this question, even though all my life I was clearly drawn to religion and theology. Without thinking about it, I said enthusiastically and to my own surprise: "Yes!"

"Okay, no problem. We can help you with that here, too," he said. I felt that a large door had opened and sunlight was pouring in. Finally, I was able to admit to myself that I had felt called to this for a very long time. The Presbyterians, who had been ordaining women since the 1950s, were open and matter-of-fact about it. They found no conflict between my intellectual interests and vocation in ministry. Unlike many other denominations, the Presbyterians understand teaching as ministry and ordain for that. I did not need to first pastor a church to get ordained; my vocation was acceptable just as it was.

My local church elected me an elder and the denomination awarded me a grant to help with educational expenses. Finally, I felt recognized, validated, and supported professionally. But now the seesaw tipped in the other direction, for on the personal side there was a lack. In this new environment, such things as nurturing, intimate community, daily involvement in each other's lives—these were much harder to find. People were cordial, but they didn't become as deeply concerned with each other as I had known in my ethnic background or in evangelicalism. Everyone was always rushing off to study, preach, or research. Connections between people seemed more task-oriented and short-term. Welcome to mainstream Protestantism.

Graduation, Ordination, Adoption

As for the infertility, Jeff and I struggled on, and, finally, after four years of tests, surgeries, therapy, and support groups, we decided to put our names with an adoption agency in New York. Several of my cousins had adopted children who fit seamlessly into the larger family, so I wasn't worried about that aspect. Jeff and I were excited about our decision and dug in for the long wait. They said it could be as much as five years.

In the meantime, I packed as much into my waiting period as I could. Mainstream Protestantism had done a good job inculturating me into its work ethic: I finished my doctoral courses, did extra work to qualify for ordination, took my four comprehensive exams *and* my five ordination exams, and researched, wrote, and defended my dissertation. My dissertation topic was considered a little offbeat, though. I had chosen to write on the Shakers, an odd topic for a theologian. Still concerned with gender issues, I wanted to understand how their Father-Mother God idea had emerged, what the theology of it was, and how it had affected the community.

With all that done—thesis, Ph.D. work, and the requirements for ordination—I graduated. My in-laws traveled to New Jersey for the big event, and my parents insisted upon a big family party in a cousin's restaurant at the Jersey shore. Driving there, my father unexpectedly pulled into a florist to buy a corsage. "Oh, you don't have to do that, Daddy," I said. "People don't wear corsages for everything anymore." With feeling, he said: "But I *want* you to have it. This is a very special day." He pinned it on the pink dress I had bought specifically for this occasion. The party dress was kind of a silly symbol, but I needed something. For after years of hippy, then preppy clothes, years of feminist sartorial restraint, years of seclusion in the library, years of financial deprivation, years of unsuccessful fertility treatments, and years of work in a traditionally male field, I needed to remind myself that I was still a woman.

A year after I graduated, I was offered a job as Assistant Professor of Theology at The Methodist Theological School in Ohio, near Columbus. With this official "call," I was now qualified to get ordained. When I told my parents about this, the best my father could say was, "Well, at least you're not becoming a nun." The ordination was held on a Sunday afternoon in Hopewell Presbyterian Church, where I was an elder. Although Kempton Hewitt, the Dean of my new school, flew out to make a speech at the event, very few of the local congregation attended. In fact, the processional held more people than the audience. Although it was a happy day for me, this spotty attendance confirmed my negative evaluation of the mainstream Protestant community.

My parents, however, were willing to attend even though the whole thing made them very uncomfortable. Their presence made me nervous, too. I consoled myself by thinking that, at least in this staid Protestant atmosphere, there weren't any statues or crucifixes to upset my mother. But it felt weird that they were watching me do something so aberrant to their backgrounds. I had no idea what they were thinking. I felt especially strange when it came time for me to serve communion—always a highlight for a new ordinand. Although intellectually I had worked it all out, emotionally I was entering uncharted territory. I felt almost dizzy when I saw my father get into the communion line. As he held out his hands, he gave me a deep look that I could not understand. I didn't know what he was trying to communicate to me, and it shook me up. But I was impressed that he would participate in a Protestant communion. The Italian Catholicism of his youth had taught him that this was a direct route to hell.

With all this going on—the graduation, job search, and ordination—I was too busy to focus on our low place on the waiting list at the adoption agency. But, overall, life was good. Jeff was satisfied with the location of my new job, figuring it would be a good employment market for him. After a slow start, he had finally begun working in computer documentation. Our marriage seemed stable now. After thirteen years of preparation with virtually no salary—helped only by part-time jobs and scholarships—I would finally start my teaching ministry. We would finally be able to save some money. We would buy a house. And some day we would have a child. Our "real" adult life was about to begin.

Waiting for David

We drove off happily to Ohio, rented a small apartment in the town of Delaware, and I settled into the faculty life of my new school, affectionately known as "Methesco." Most of the predominantly older male faculty had been there since the school was founded, and yet they were supportive and accepting of newcomers. Neither gender-biased like the evangelical world nor hierarchical like the Ivy League, Methesco was small, unpretentious, and friendly.

Clearly, though, I still retained some of my bicoastal bias, for I missed the ethnicity and stimulation of the East Coast, the vibrant oddness of Berkeley, and especially the ocean. After all, New Yorkers and Californians habitually dismissed everything between the Atlantic and Pacific as the "fly-over zone." I also missed friends and family. We had no relatives within an easy drive, and this put us at a disadvantage in the family-oriented Midwest. On weekends, everyone but us seemed to have extended-family plans. But because our apartment in Ohio was exactly 560 miles from my parents' house in New Jersey, we had to wait for major holidays and summers to see my relatives. Jeff's were equally far away.

Every time I visited New Jersey, one of my cousins would ask, "When are you going to come back home? Couldn't you just get a job here?" They all seemed to think it was my choice to live away from them, something I could rectify easily. I had tried repeatedly to find a job on the East Coast with no success, something I continued to do for years. Yet, I wondered, too. Didn't God believe in family? Why, when I followed God, did it seem to lead me further away from my roots?

I noted that many of our students were willing to move away from extended family in order to pursue their call to ministry. I was impressed at how they often gave up lucrative careers, sold houses, packed up belongings, moved spouses and children to follow their vocation. Unfortunately, the impermanence of their lives would only continue if they were ordained in the United Methodist Church, since Methodist ministers had to "itinerate," that is, be moved around from church to church within their "conference" every few years by their superiors. I knew the denomination had its reasons, but giving up permanency of community seemed to me a hard thing to ask of ministers—so different from the vision I had inherited from the Jews and Italians.

Being with people who considered this situation normal only heightened my own feelings of loneliness and disconnection. My academic work was going well, but I was still waiting to establish a real home and family. Since we considered the apartment temporary, we hung no pictures on the wall, no curtains on the windows. We spent weekends househunting but found nothing we both liked that we could afford on my assistant professor salary. I was discouraged that

Jeff was still not working. He was at a disadvantage, because his résumé was spotty. Nevertheless, he rejected the job offers he did receive, insisting they were beneath him.

Then one evening in early May we got a phone call that would completely change my understanding of connectedness and family and "home." It was a call from our social worker at the adoption agency. "We have a little five-week-old boy for you. How soon can you drive back here and see him?" Like many other prospective adoptive parents, we had not fixed up the nursery yet, almost as though it would prolong or even "jinx" our chances. However, within two days someone had given us a crib, we had acquired other basic equipment, and we were traveling down the Pennsylvania Turnpike toward the East Coast. After a night at my parents' house, we drove to Manhattan and were taken into a little reception room upstairs in the agency building. Our social worker sat with us while the foster parents brought the baby in. He was a beautiful infant with blue eyes, blond hair, and cute little features. He weighed about ten pounds, and was dressed in a tiny tuxedo.

"We call him Peanut," the foster mother said. "He is the cutest, sweetest baby we've ever cared for, and he can sleep through anything." His birth mother had chosen us after reading our profile and seeing our pictures. She wanted a family that emphasized education and religion. The social worker and foster parents left us alone with the baby for a few minutes so we could decide, but it was just a formality. When the social worker and foster parents returned, we asked a few dazed questions, trying to seem on top of things. Then they asked for the tuxedo back "for the next little boy." The baby was completely undressed and given to us without even a diaper on, so we could start from scratch. We nervously dressed him, put him in the car seat, and drove back to my parents' house.

Baby David was welcomed like a little prince and seemed quite content to be with us. It didn't take long for us to bond. It was so clear that he was a gift from God, and we especially appreciated him after all the time and effort. But we were happy now. The next day we drove back to Ohio. Since there was no leave policy for new parents at my school, I had to get back to my classes. Jeff still had not found a job, so he stayed home with the baby. His day was consumed with bottles and diapers, but he seemed very happy. Soon he was boasting that he was "the real mother," and I was inept. Although Jeff was doing a good job and I felt fortunate, his words really hurt me. As an adoptive mother, I felt insecure about my role and felt at a disadvantage, having to leave for work with a baby in the home. But after six months, Jeff took a job and we found someone to look after the baby while I was in class. That's when things changed.

No Promised Land

Although we had gotten here by a lengthy, circuitous, and unconventional route, our dream was almost complete. Why then, at this very point, did our life begin to unravel? First I noticed that Jeff was beginning to drink heavily. When I checked in the basement, I saw that the bottles we stored there for special occasions disappeared quickly. Every evening he brought home a six-pack of beer and would sit in front of the TV, drinking and incommunicative. Then he became obsessed with hygiene, order, and routine. He seemed to always be angry, and maligned all my efforts, still saying he was "the real mother" of David. He began to overreact to the predictable bumps in daily family life. One day as I was drying David's hair with a towel, Jeff got impatient, grabbed a hair dryer and turned it up full speed. Instead of stopping when the baby cried, he started yelling at both of us. Another time, David's bedroom door got locked by accident. As David cried from his crib inside, I stood outside the door, reassuring him and trying to figure out how to open it. When I called to Jeff for help, he got enraged, ran outside, and drove off.

I felt desperate, helpless, and panicky. As I had done earlier, I began to hide in my work. At least this was something I could control, and it felt stabilizing. So, besides caring for David and teaching, I put in several hours a week working hard to ready my manuscript for publication. I felt guilty for taking time away from the household, yet, other than my times alone with David, I felt most free when I worked on that book. It was something completely mine and it gave me renewed energy.

I began seeing a therapist and urged Jeff to do the same. He refused, saying I was the one with the problem. We limped along like this for two years, celebrating David's second birthday and doing the usual domestic things. But Jeff began acting and talking even more strangely. He warned of getting into a car accident and once threatened to get a gun. He drove erratically, even stopping in the middle of a busy highway one night, screaming at me.

Ever since my broken arm several years ago—which both our families knew about—no one had inquired whether the violence continued. There had been other incidents—although none as serious—but I had not told anyone. We lived far from family now, and I did not think they could help. Nor did I mention the situation to anyone at school. After all, Jeff and I had come here as a happily married couple. Indeed, the Dean had said we would be good role models for the students. In addition, we lived in a small town where everyone gossiped, and every police call was reported in the local paper. I was afraid of jeopardizing my job and, worse, losing David. When the therapist told me that, if I ever mentioned a violent incident, he would have to report it to the police, I stopped seeing him.

One night I was sitting at the kitchen table while Jeff washed dishes. I had given up doing such things when Jeff was around, since he often followed behind me and redid the task or complained about my work. Nor did I feel free to leave the room, since Jeff would accuse me of being lazy. So, paralyzed, I sat there trying to make conversation about a needed purchase. "Jeff, I don't know if we should buy a new computer. Our old one is a problem, but they are so expensive," I said. With his back to me, Jeff angrily retorted, "Stop worrying about money all the time. Just buy the damn computer."

"But I don't know . . . they're expensive," I reiterated. Suddenly, Jeff turned around, walked over to me, and put his wet hands around my neck, dragging me out of my chair. I tried to move away from him and managed to fall on the floor. In the process, Jeff's hands came off my neck, but he went over to the sink and began to throw the dirty dishwater on me. I got up and stared him in the eye as hard as I could. All the memories of previous incidents, his anger, and my helplessness suddenly solidified in me. "You're not going to do this anymore," I said as fiercely as I could.

Once I had resolved to change things (though I wasn't yet sure how), things began to happen in my life to support my decision. First, I was awarded tenure—a development hastened by three years of good performance, a year's credit for previous experience, and the imminent publication of my book. Then, that same spring, David's adoption was finalized, which further impressed upon me the need to create a safe, abuse-free home environment. Finally, I hinted at my family situation to a therapist who occasionally taught courses on addiction at my school. She urged me to resume therapy and also let me know there was a domestic violence support group in the next county.

I began to attend the domestic violence support group. A social worker I met there also began giving me some private counseling. She would meet me in the local police station to ensure protection and confidentiality. During one session, she showed me a list of signs that abusers would manifest. I was especially struck by one that read: "Feigns conversion." I felt a chill and said, "Wait a minute. That's when I decided to marry him, when he became a Christian." She looked at me with skepticism and pity, and said, "This is very common." I pushed back my feelings of panic and focused on the other signs. Enough of them matched my own situation to convince me I was in more danger than I realized.

At the support group, the other members said I would eventually have to leave Jeff. I didn't want to hear or believe this. I wanted to learn how to stand up to him—not leave him. Nevertheless, those women who had already left abusive mates spent much time trying to convince the rest of us there was no other way. The several other Christians in the group were as paralyzed and guilt-ridden as I was. I was scared now and paid close attention to the life-saving strategies they taught us. We were told to be ready for anything; leave a spare set of car keys somewhere; always have some money in another location; have some diapers and baby clothes in the car.

Most important, the counselor taught us to go public. "Now, I realize you will feel ashamed and afraid when the violence starts," she said. "You will want to hide. But this is the last thing you should do. Go outside, start screaming, and call attention to yourself. I don't care if you are embarrassed. This is a protective action for you. You want the police. You want the neighbors. This will save your life." I saw the logic, but it frightened me. After all, I was a minister and seminary professor in a small town with a paper that reported every police call, a paper that everyone read.

Still hoping that the marriage could be repaired—after all, God had brought us together and would surely not desert us now—I resumed therapy with a different therapist, an ordained minister and trained counselor who, I thought, could understand our situation better. I told him I was afraid of Jeff and about the history of violence in our marriage. He urged me to invite Jeff to join us. Jeff—although continuing to insist I was the one with problems—finally agreed to attend just a few sessions. At the second joint session, the counselor confronted Jeff and said, "What we really have to deal with, before we go any further, is the violence."

Jeff turned white but said nothing. Instead he jumped up, ran out the door, got into his car, floored the engine, and sped out of the parking lot. After a few moments of stunned silence, the counselor said, "Well, I guess it's just us now. What do you want to talk about?" I was incredulous. "Wait a minute," I said in a panic. "You have your nice safe home to go to after this. But I have to go back to our apartment, and I'm afraid." Nothing much was said after that. The session ended and I left, shaken and petrified.

I didn't know what else to do, so I went to the sitter's, picked up David, and went home. In a controlled panic, I baked some chicken for dinner and waited. Jeff came home at the usual time, agitated with repressed rage. I got the dinner served, put David in his high chair, and we began to silently eat. I sat still and said nothing, praying that things would not escalate, but knowing they easily could. I didn't have to wait long. Suddenly, David spit some chicken skin out of his mouth.

"Yucky, no like this," he said. Jeff jumped up. "You are going to eat your food," he said loudly to the toddler. David began crying, and I realized I could no longer calmly sit there and eat. The tension was explosive. I was distraught and began again the endless loop that had been running in my head for weeks now: "*This sweet baby, he's so innocent. He shouldn't have to go through this. This isn't right. We promised to give him love. Look at him, just sitting there unaware of what is really happening.*" It all seemed so pathetic, so tragic, and so wrong.

I tried to assess the situation, as I had been taught by the support group. Jeff looked so tightly wound, almost robotic as he ate his food, with a rage-filled expression, burning eyes focused on his plate. If I didn't act, something horrible was going to happen. Suddenly, all the advice and training kicked in. I was scared enough to do what they had urged, even if it meant humiliation and exposure. Unfastening David's high-chair tray, I picked him up and walked toward the door.

"Where are you going?" Jeff demanded angrily. Then he glared at me and said, in a slow, controlled, but very threatening monotone that sent panic through my body: "You are not going anywhere. We are going to eat. You cannot go outside." I took a deep breath and said, as lightly as I could manage, "Oh, we're just going to get some air, it's stuffy in here." It was August and, as usual, hot in Central Ohio. I walked toward the door and opened it. Then, with David in my arms, I started across the parking lot toward my car.

Within seconds, Jeff came rushing outside after us and tried to wrestle the baby from my arms. As I tried to hang onto him, David started crying loudly, and I started screaming. Jeff continued yelling at me as doors opened and neighbors stuck their heads out. After a few seconds, Jeff wrested David away and ran back inside the apartment. My next-door neighbor looked at me in shock and then asked, "What do you want me to do?" As I had been counseled, I told her "Please call the police."

The domestic violence classes had stressed one thing:

Don't leave the child. If it came down to a court issue, they said, you would be suspect if you protected yourself but left your child behind. Since Jeff was back inside with the baby, I went back inside, too. I was re-entering the equivalent of a burning building and might not come out again, but the decision was obvious. This baby was a gift, and I was going to protect him no matter what. Soon the police arrived. Jeff was very angry when he opened the door and saw them. The police went in and assessed the situation, telling me to wait outside. By now, David was back in his high chair, and Jeff would not let him out.

I heard loud voices and arguing, then the police came back outside. "We can see that this situation is volatile. He could get violent. We advise you to come with us, and we'll take you to the shelter," one officer said. I knew I couldn't do this and tried to explain: "I can't leave without the baby. Can't you get him for me?" One officer went back in for a few seconds, but came out without David. Turning to me, he said: "Look, lady, it's his baby, too. And we can't make any arrests because we haven't witnessed any violence. But if you don't come with us now, we wash our hands of the case. We don't take any responsibility for what could happen." I felt more abandoned than I ever had. But, still, the decision was obvious. I looked him in the eye and said: "I won't leave without the baby." Looking disgusted, the police left.

Before going back inside, though, I asked that same neighbor to call the therapist friend. I knew she and her husband were active in the Alcoholics Anonymous community, and they had intervened in other crisis situations. Fortunately, she had insisted that I memorize her number. My neighbor agreed to do this, and I went back in. Once we were alone again, Jeff began to berate me loudly. I sat quietly in the living room, praying my friends would come soon. When they arrived, they looked over the situation and insisted I put

David to bed while they spoke with Jeff. When I came back down forty-five minutes later, they were just finishing their conversation. As they stood up to leave, they said to me: "We think things will be okay tonight. Jeff might come with us to an AA meeting tomorrow. Give us a call in the morning, Linda."

I didn't want them to leave me alone with Jeff. But David was asleep finally, and I had to stay. I actually slept in the same bed with Jeff that night, staying right on the edge of the mattress, tense and scared. Before falling asleep, Jeff said to me, in that same controlled, slow, threatening monotone, "That wasn't good what you did. You should not have called the police. You should not have done that. This isn't going to be good. The problem is your work. You just won't be able to write any more books or give speeches. That's it."

Then he fell asleep and I stayed awake, freezing cold, shaking. My mind was racing, as it often did when something was wrong and I couldn't figure it out. *"Is my work the main problem? How can I give it up? I do feel guilty. But how can it be wrong? It's a gift from God. I'm sure of it. It makes me feel like me. I thought Jeff supported me in this. What's happened?"*

Dream Ends

In the morning, Jeff simply got up and left for work. I stayed in bed until I heard his car pull away. I was amazed that he had left me alone with the baby, because I knew what I had to do. I called the friend who had come over last night, and she advised me to get some help from my colleagues. So I called a friend on the faculty, and she alerted several others. Before long, four fellow teachers, including the new Dean, arrived with a small pickup truck. They sized up the situation and asked me what I wanted to take. I tried to answer, but could only cry. So, several of them went inside and decided for me. As they went back and forth from apartment to truck, I stood near the door, stunned and speechless, watching them and watching David. The toddler was completely oblivious to the situation, but ran happily around us, dirty diaper and all.

Once the truck was loaded, my colleagues debated where I should stay and with whom. I still stood by helplessly, not knowing what would be best. I didn't think this could really be happening, but, of course, it was. Finally, they decided I should go home with the Dean. He was the only one with a house and attached garage. That way, there would be no trace of me, should Jeff try to find us. The things my colleagues had decided to take for me—my stereo, some clothes, and furniture that they decided I liked and needed—they would put in another colleague's small garage at her apartment complex.

As I locked the door, I wondered what Jeff would think when he came home. Then I buckled David in his car seat and followed the Dean's car with mine. "*This is brave of him,*" I thought, as the Dean drove away. Although mostly in shock, I was grateful to all of them and impressed that they had done this for me. True to form, I also felt very guilty.

Chapter Nine

Three Flavors of Guilt

Victims of domestic violence often blame themselves. I know this now, but I did not know it then. One thing is certain, however. I was certainly set up for self-blame. Even before I got married, my emotional interior was like a carton of Neapolitan ice cream, with its three flavors side-by-side: the two flavors of guilt I inherited, Jewish and Catholic, alongside my adopted flavor of Protestantism. Added in, like chocolate chips, were my feminist convictions which, ironically, brought their own share of self-doubt. As a final touch, popular theories from psychology and addiction recovery were the colorful candy sprinkles topping it off. Just dig in anywhere.

My Jewish mother had once said: "If you knew how to handle Jeff better, you'd have a perfectly good husband." She didn't mind that Jeff was critical of me—in fact, they often agreed on what was wrong. My Catholic father didn't believe in violence, but family came first, so he abhorred divorce. He could allow that I had made a mistake once and had to get divorced, but this time he felt certain Jeff and I would get back together, especially now that we had a child. The Protestants I knew prized individual autonomy over preservation of the family. According to that ethos, I had an obligation to leave if I were being repressed and restricted.

My feminist friends talked with quiet horror of the mis-guided women who fell for violent men. According to them, even when a woman was taken by surprise, she should—at the very first inkling—leave immediately and never look back. Commonly accepted psychological theory asserted that if a woman got into a violent relationship, she had most likely been abused in her parental home and was drawn to dys-functional men. And the reigning ethos among recovering alcoholics was that the female partner of an alcoholic was just as sick, if not sicker, than her mate—her fault was "en-abling" him.

Even though my intellect and experience contradicted many of these guilt inducers—and several of these posi-tions contradicted each other—they all managed to chase me around an endless, convoluted maze, with no way out. When I ran from one type of blame, I encountered another equally judgmental monster around the next turn. I was not sure how much I was a victim and how much a sinner. So even though I was away from the violence, I could find no emotional peace.

At least David and I were physically safe, though. We stayed with the Dean and his wife for a week. I felt grateful to them for making room for us. I don't know how well my gratitude came across. I think I was too distraught to ex-press much of anything in particular. But they acted rather matter-of-fact about it, as if it were no trouble to put up a distressed colleague and her toddler son. While their behav-ior was in keeping with the other lifelong Protestants I knew, low-key and reserved, I knew grace when I saw it.

Our classes for fall were about to start, but the Dean feared my situation was still unsafe. He excused me from the first week so I could get out of the area for awhile. A colleague temporarily took my classes, and David and I drove east to my parents in New Jersey. Just like a yo-yo, I always reverted back there. This time it was much different, however. They no longer lived on Bloomfield Avenue but had moved to a tiny house at the Jersey shore.

A few years back, wanting to retire, they had sold the bakery and all the equipment to a young Italian couple just starting out. Because the couple could not get financing, my parents held the mortgage themselves. They had high hopes that the business they had worked so hard to build would continue. Since they still owned the building, they continued to live above the shop. But, a few months after the sale, when my parents returned from a celebratory winter trip to Florida, they found the bakery deserted, all the equipment gone, burst pipes, rotting cakes everywhere, and a floor covered in ice. In the end—after my parents cleaned up the mess themselves—the business was bought up for very little money by a developer who turned it into a laundromat.

When David and I arrived, my parents did not know what to do or say. They did not need another tragedy, but I knew they would never turn us away. Going there may have not been the wisest choice, however, for if Jeff decided to track me down, it was the first place he'd look. Fortunately, I didn't see or hear from him. I later learned from the therapist friend, the one who had calmed Jeff down the night before I left, that Jeff was now attending AA meetings.

Although both my parents had come from "broken homes," they had no experience with alcoholism or violence. Nor had there been any divorces among that generation in the family. They seemed almost incredulous that things could have been *that* bad, and I found myself struggling to convince them, which made me feel guilty and strange. After a week, I decided to take my chances and return to Ohio. Once I arrived back, I felt too panicky to live again in our apartment or even drive down that street. I asked our seminary President if we could stay temporarily in campus housing. He

said we could be there for a few weeks until I found somewhere else.

A colleague suggested I get a restraining order that would
include the campus. She insisted on driving me to a lawyer
the day after I arrived. The attorney said that the only way
I could get the order was to file for divorce. I wasn't ready
to take that step, but—with my colleague urging me on—
I felt compelled to sign the papers just to get the protection. It was clear that my colleague, like my other feminist
friends, thought I was crazy to believe the situation could
be repaired.

Life in the Safe Lane

Back at seminary, I settled into teaching classes. I worried,
as I had done years ago at Regent, that people would judge
me. After all, I taught from a feminist perspective and was
known as a successful professional in a good marriage.
When I was hired, the previous Dean had said I would be a
role model for my female students. So I feared that not only
would my image be destroyed, but I might be the source of
disillusionment to the students.

To my relief, I found support instead of judgment. What
I had forgotten to factor in was that many of our students
had started seminary after their own personal crises, including divorce. There were lots of single parents on campus, and they understood my situation immediately. Many
came forward to share their own stories of trauma and pain.
Every day I would find anonymous notes and greeting cards
pushed under my door, assuring me of God's love, of their
love, and encouraging me to keep going. I don't know what
people said when I wasn't around, but to my face I only encountered respect, discretion, and care.

As for the faculty and staff, mostly they regarded my situation realistically and compassionately. However, I also sensed an undertow of somewhat politicized attitudes that ranged from male colleagues who hinted that my feminist ideology had not helped my marriage, to female colleagues who were impatient that I balked at divorce. Their signals were subtle but enough to prolong the counterproductive guilt loops going around in my head. After all, I was a feminist who had established an egalitarian marriage with Jeff. Domestic violence was the complete antithesis of this. How could it have happened?

It didn't take much to get my religious guilt going, either. The evangelicals had taught me to put a high value on family. They spoke ominously about "the breakdown of the American family" and insisted that Christians should be different. They had counseled me that God could forgive me for my first failed marriage, because I was not yet "saved." But I didn't have that excuse this time. How could *this* marriage— so clearly arranged by God—end? I wanted to believe that, when there was enough faith and trust in God, miracles could happen. Why were none happening now?

Even the book that I had worked on during the worst of my marriage crisis—the project that had provided me with an emotional lifeline—got appropriated by my guilt-making. *Gender, Doctrine and God: The Shakers and Contemporary Theology* was published at about the same time that my separation agreement was finalized. My joy was tempered by worry that all my hard work had somehow contributed to the marital distress. I'm sure that is what Jeff would claim. And I fell into guilty agreement far too easily.

Jeff's visitation rights also added to my worries. A schedule was set up so that David could see his dad. Some friends argued I should completely restrict this, but I knew the court would not be sympathetic. After all, there was no public record of the violence. Also, I decided that—especially since David was adopted—it would be better for him to have a troubled father who loved him than to lose such an important attachment. However, I worried about the effect of Jeff's agitated state on the toddler. Every time David went off on a visit, I remained anxious until he was home again.

Each time I saw Jeff, I hoped for some sign that things were improving. He continued to attend AA and I went to Al-Anon. I did not think alcoholism was the foundational problem, but Jeff seemed content to leave it there. He continued to berate me by phone and in person—one time loudly declaiming in the middle of a McDonald's that he was like Christ and I was like the Roman soldiers. I was afraid to be near him, even though we met only in public places.

My housing situation remained in limbo for months. I still paid the rent on our apartment although it was unoccupied. I had tried several times to return to it, but each time I went inside, my heart would pound and I would feel dizzy. I couldn't stay more than a few minutes. Although I did look at other apartments, anywhere but campus felt very unsafe. After several months of this and with friends' help, I packed everything up, moved it to a storage bin, and gave up the apartment. Our campus stay stretched out to a year and a half.

I didn't want a divorce, but could see no reason to stop the process. Continuing in limbo seemed worse. So, more than a year after the separation, the divorce was finalized on a cold, gray December day that completely mirrored my mood. I thought the court would at least listen to my reports of violence, but when I tried to tell the magistrate about it, he interrupted me and said, "I don't want to hear about your personal problems." I was awarded full custody of David, but liberal visitation privileges were given to Jeff. That day I was empty and completely drained. The process had been one long burial of the dream, shovelful by shovelful.

Healing in Winter

By then I had earned my first short sabbatical and was off from teaching for one quarter. I was awarded a research grant from the Association of Theological Schools and was invited to be a fellow at the Ecumenical Institute in Collegeville, Minnesota. David and I left for Minnesota right after the court date. I knew it would be good place for us. Located on the campus of St. John's University and Abbey, the Institute provided a ready-made community of scholars, mutual encouragement for our writing, and the opportunity to participate in the restorative Benedictine atmosphere. Even though it was bitter cold and frozen when we arrived, I was relieved to be out of Ohio.

David and I had plenty of uninterrupted time together. Each day I got up while it was still dark and wrote for four or five hours before he awoke. He was nearly four now, so on the days I had seminars or library research to do, he would go to a nearby nursery school. Most evenings it was just the two of us at home, cooking hot dogs in the fireplace, watching videos, playing with Legos. On weekends we would visit libraries and museums, bundle up to watch the ice-fishing, or sled and skate. Although Jeff had several sisters in towns nearby where he could have stayed, he never came up to visit. As a result, David and I both calmed down and started to feel normal again.

While at St. John's I chose to research the topic of addiction from a theological perspective. It was a logical choice for several reasons. Our school had a degree in Alcohol and Drug Abuse Ministry, and many of our seminary students were recovering alcoholics. The students often claimed that

"Twelve Steps" was good theology and the meetings more spiritually satisfying than church. I wanted to understand why they—like Jeff—could become so evangelistic about the program. In addition, two committed AA members had intervened in our marital situation. Thanks to them, Jeff had become extremely active in AA, even mentoring others. But I thought his drinking was a minor problem compared to the violence, which only happened when he was sober. I worried that AA was too focused on alcoholism to be able to address this serious issue.

Minnesota, the "land of ten thousand treatment centers," was the perfect place to study addiction recovery. I visited Hazelden and other therapeutic centers. But I also visited several domestic violence agencies, to see what kind of overlap or disjunctions occurred between the two problems. I wanted to come up with an adequate theological understanding of sin and victimization. Eventually all this resulted in my third book, *Victims & Sinners: Spiritual Roots of Addiction and Recovery.*

As I worked, I began to see that the addiction-recovery movement—although very helpful for people whose primary problem was alcoholism and drug abuse—was becoming a very large umbrella to cover many diverse problems. The Twelve Step philosophy had become practically an alternative spirituality replacing deeper and richer analyses of the human condition. Many diverse problems that had formerly been considered either crime or sin had been moved to the category of disease.

I appreciated that the technique was practical and that many people found God through it. But I saw others who blamed religion for their feelings of shame and isolation. An alternative community had been set up, one that was "spiritual but not religious." Recovery could become a world unto itself, as many members got divorced and then married other recovering alcoholics, or restricted their friendships and socializing to the "recovering community." Therefore, what could have been a unifying theme instead often alienated people from religion and perpetuated the divide.

As for the church, it often provided space for meetings but offered little direct ministry to recovering persons. There may have been some judgmentalism here—but not entirely. Clergy worried about breaking the anonymity of members, and also sensed the recovery movement's alienation from organized religion. As a result, the long spiritual tradition of Christianity—which had dealt for centuries with the broader "human predicament" suffered by everyone—was not available to recovering persons. In the end, even though the program and the church were concerned about similar life problems, there was little cross-fertilization.

In my study of domestic violence, I interviewed workers in the shelter movement, and took some training as a volunteer. I learned that, although addiction was often present in violent relationships, many times men used alcohol and drugs to provide a cover for their abusive behavior. Women sometimes used such substances simply to anesthetize themselves from the pain. So just treating the addiction was not going to deal with the underlying issues.

I was especially enlightened by a man who ran a group for males convicted of domestic violence. I asked him what hope there might be for men with this problem. He said, "Oh, I've seen some improvement." Feeling hopeful and encouraged, I asked him, "Oh, really? How much healing do you see?" But my relief faded when he said, with a laugh, "Well, we just return them to the normal types of male dominance that the rest of men in our society practice. They still act controlling, but without the overt violence."

The research, interviews, and volunteer training helped me come to terms with my shame. I saw that even an intelligent, independent, and religious person could be caught in the trap of violence. My cultural training as a woman had encouraged me to avoid facing reality. My father had protected me so much that I assumed all men were trustworthy. And, ironically, my pride in achieving professional success kept me from acknowledging that I could still be a victim. In the end, however, it became clear that domestic violence—like addiction—is not simply an individual psychological problem, but something that requires society's recognition and cooperation before incidences can be reduced. I also began to see a glimmer of God's grace. For what had begun as a personal problem was now an impetus for my research and writing. Without planning it, I began to get invitations to speak and write on these topics. I realized there was a way to find meaning in what I had survived.

Starting Over Again

Once my sabbatical at the Ecumenical Institute ended, I returned to Ohio. That's where my job was, and it was the only real anchor we had. We moved into a townhouse apartment, just David and I, two biologically unrelated people, bound together by love and circumstance. I set about trying to create as normal and happy a life as possible. We planted flowers, bought outdoor furniture and a gas grill (welcome to suburbia), had friends over for dinner, made parties, took trips, and visited my family in New Jersey. I also brought David to seminary with me frequently—even to my classes sometimes—so he could feel he had a bigger home and people who welcomed him, just as I had had in the bakery.

All this activity helped keep despair and depression at bay. I couldn't let this sweet little boy down. To have him bouncing along holding my hand gave me bursts of joy. The effort to create a happy life for him had the side benefit of creating one for me. I began to realize that God can use whatever a person truly loves to bring that person into the light of God's love. It's part of the lure of God. Following the tiny bits of light that we see helps God move us out of the dark tunnel of despair. It was a very slow recovery, however, with the guilt and self-blame leaving me in steady if small increments.

It helped that I had the addiction book to work on. Finally, so I could finish it, the Louisville Institute awarded me a grant, I took a year without pay, and accepted the invitation to join the Center of Theological Inquiry at Princeton for that period. While on the East Coast, David started first grade, got baptized, and visited his adoption agency in Manhattan. I had always wanted to show him the place where we had picked him up. I wasn't sure that he was old enough to find the meeting meaningful, but it was very healing for me. With some trepidation, I explained to Gretchen, our original social worker, what had happened in the intervening years. I was afraid she would be judgmental, but instead she said: "We know these things happen sometimes. You are not the first. When you were here you met the qualifications. Don't feel guilty about this anymore." Without knowing it, she gave absolution and benediction, thus freeing me from one more bit of guilt. As for David, he began swaggering around saying "I'm a New Yorker," and seemed quite pleased about it.

The following year we returned to Ohio. Shortly after that, my parents started to decline. First my father became ill. Because he wanted to stay at home, health-care workers were hired. After several years of increasing debilitation, my father was hospitalized. He hung on there for several months, and we were away when he finally died. When I got the sad call from my brother, the funeral home had already been chosen and relatives notified. My mother and brother, though, had no plans to involve the church. When I suggested that we give him a funeral mass at the local parish, as Catholics normally have (after all, my father had never given up his Catholic roots), my mother vetoed the idea. Fortunately, we came to a compromise. At my urging, the funeral director was able to find a retired monsignor who was willing to put in an appearance at the funeral home and simply "say a blessing." My mother didn't like the idea, but she allowed it.

The family expected me to give the eulogy—which has to be one of the harder things a person does for her parent. I used 1 Corinthians 13, the "love passage," for if there was anything that characterized my father, it was his patience, generosity, and love. When the short service was over, we all went to the cemetery. Bundled up against the cold, the family took seats alongside the coffin, while the others stood behind.

After a few words from the funeral director at the gravesite, he lifted up the large crucifix which the priest had left with him to adorn the coffin, and then the folded American flag lying beside it that indicated my father was a veteran. The director reached over to offer these items to my mother. Her reaction was stark and unexpected. With an angry look on her face, she reached out her right hand to accept the flag while simultaneously and abruptly pushing the crucifix away with the back of her left hand. The funeral director paused, leaning forward, momentarily at a loss. "*You* take it," my mother said, out of the side of her mouth brusquely, without looking at me. So I did.

After the funeral, when I returned to my work and tried to write, I found I was completely blocked and could not do it. But I remembered what Patrick Henry, director of the Ecumenical Institute, had once told me: "When you're blocked," he said, "write about the block." So I found myself writing about my parents' "mixed marriage" and how the funeral had seemed to promote some kind of a further healing, at least for me. My musings soon turned into an article, which was published in a popular mainstream Protestant publication, *The Christian Century*. I received so many positive comments about it—it seemed to prompt readers to reflect more deeply on their own family situations—that the article became the inspiration for this book.

Unfortunately, it was not long before my mother began to decline as well. My brother insisted she move to a retirement center where she could have company and care. Eventually she relented but insisted it at least be somewhere that had a significant number of Jewish residents. The retirement home we found was attractive, expensive, and filled with activities. However, my mother rarely attended any of the activities and soon was staying in her room most of the time, resuming the reclusive life begun when my father became ill. When summer came, David and I drove back to New Jersey to see how she was doing. We spent a week there, and she seemed to be relatively healthy and stable. I accompanied her to a doctor visit during this time. The gerontologist addressed all his remarks to me, as though my mother—sitting there in her wheelchair but completely aware—were out of it.

The doctor announced that my mother had "end-stage emphysema." I had not heard this before. She had not indicated she was having breathing problems and all her life had distrusted doctors, keeping visits to a minimum. Although I was concerned for her health, I was especially worried about the effect of his remarks on her emotional state. I tried to get the doctor to at least address her directly. "Doctor," I said. "My mother is right here and just as sharp as ever." The doctor turned to her and asked if she had any questions.

Looking at him for the first time, she said, "What can you do for me?" With a surprisingly genial tone, he said, "Well, really, Mrs. Mercadante, you've already outlived your life expectancy." My mother seemed to shrink in her chair, looking instantly deflated and distraught. Finally, she asked, with panic in her voice, "Isn't there *anything* you can do?" He smiled and said reassuringly: "Oh, don't worry, we have a few more tricks up our sleeve. You'll get to spend many more holidays with your family."

David and I left, but, only a week later, I got a call from my brother saying that our mother had died in her sleep. I found myself once again rushing back and being asked to do a eulogy. My brother wanted to make sure my mother had a Jewish ceremony. He learned that there was a rabbi at the retirement center who was available to officiate. But when we called him, the rabbi was surprised to learn that my mother had been Jewish. With her Italian last name and failure to connect with people there or attend services, he had never even met her. He agreed it was better if I did the eulogy, since he hadn't known her. But this eulogy was much more difficult to compose. The audience would be a mixture of Christians and Jews, and I didn't feel free to focus on the afterlife. Finally I decided to focus on the fact that, in spite of difficulties, my mother had never abandoned her faith.

The day after the funeral, I received a call from my brother. He requested that I go over to our mother's apartment and take whatever I wanted before he had it cleared out. We met there and went upstairs in the elevator. I found it very hard to enter the room. Once inside, I felt frozen and distraught; I could barely focus and took very little. It was clear to me that something was ending. On all my many trips to New Jersey, I had always stayed with my parents. Now there was no house, no invitations, and no home base. I had always been ambivalent about New Jersey—running away from it as much as I ricocheted back. But losing it was harder than I expected.

Losing New Jersey

A complicated mixture of motives had led me away from familial and geographic roots. So many things contributed: a need for self-development, an inchoate desire to escape ethnic constraints, the discomfort of my religious confusion, and my burgeoning career aspirations. The increasing mobility of American life, the equal rights movement, and the liberating atmosphere of the 1970s also contributed. All these conditions and influences—with my mixed ethnic and religious background the most prominent—had made me anxious to find wholeness within myself.

Ultimately, however, it became clear that wholeness is something only God can provide. I had simply responded to the lure of God. God reached out to me and drew me along an often misty and rocky path. I was hungry and needy, a condition that makes the divine work a lot easier. Even though following this lure had been disruptive, confusing, and sometimes painful, I could not resist it. For me, this path proved the only way to unity and joy. Divine grace also supplied an essential insight: Happiness and joy are not the same. Wholeness does bring an undercurrent of the security and peace we call joy, but it often comes at the cost of simple contentment. In fact, the trajectory of joy and of sadness can often cross paths on the journey toward wholeness.

I had just lost my parents and my extended family as a functioning unit. I had finally left New Jersey for good. No matter what remnants of East Coast provincialism and ethnic identity lingered, Ohio would have to be home for now. I obviously would never have "the perfect Christian family" or anything that my early hopes included. David would never live in an intact family, there would be no siblings for him, and the dream would never be realized. Was the dream I had carried simply a residue from 1950s family "togetherness," a romanticizing of ethnic identity, or was it in fact something real and valuable but rapidly fading in our society?

I felt sure that God must be in favor of all these things: family, self-development, spiritual growth, and service. I noticed it wasn't true for everyone in the ministry that they had to leave family in order to follow God. I could see that many had their own intact families, relatives nearby, and their work as well. But I knew I had to make the most of what I did have. I bought a house in a community about fifteen miles from my seminary with an excellent school system. David was about to enter middle school, so he and I chose the house together. Finally, after all these years, I had a house.

Although I was very worried about the obligations, soon we learned how to cut grass, plant things, and do maintenance. Fortunately, a former student of mine, an older minister, became our adopted uncle, and did everything we couldn't. David and I got involved in things outside seminary and church, in the wider community. We joined clubs and met new people. In the meantime, David's dad married someone he had met in the Twelve Step program and moved nearby. David now had two homes and a wider network of family. In the end, it took a long time to get to our version of "normal." Our journey didn't follow any idealized script. But at least we made it.

The Reluctant Protestant

The way I see it, I'm not exactly a poster child for the "victorious Christian life." That's my image of the ideal believer, sailing through all manner of crises, with faith and attitude intact. I know, of course, that I've had some advantages, good experiences, and modest career success. I also know God is responsible for much growth. Even so, my close friends tell me I still act as if I expect Cossacks to ride into the *shtetl* in the middle of the night, looking for the hidden Jews.

Although I have achieved things I never even dreamed of when I lived on Bloomfield Avenue, on many days I'm just a reluctant Protestant. I miss so many things from my past: boisterous Italian family dinners, smart Jewish humor, playing on the beach with my cousins, warm evangelical community—in fact, sometimes I even miss Newark! I've certainly managed to find some success in this Protestant world, since I am now a theologian, an ordained Presbyterian, and a committed believer. But I don't think I've achieved a complete personality transplant. I guess I'll never be the archetypal WASP: low-key, calm, moderately pious, guilt-free, self-confident, and decisive.

On the other hand, I speculate that deep down no one is really like that, for when we peel off the layers of our personality styles, cultural backgrounds, childhood issues, and current baggage, we find a human condition characterized by a pervasive anxiety. None of us sails through life on a perpetually calm sea, and even when our boat is seaworthy, we get anxious anyway. As Saint Augustine said, our hearts *are* truly restless until they rest in God. Spiritually, we all have ADD (Attention Deficit Disorder), finding it nearly impossible to focus on the one thing that really matters. So if God didn't keep the divine arms around us, we'd never get any rest at all.

As for the church, I've seen its many varieties and guises and have often found safe harbor there. I could never say I'm "spiritual but not religious," for I believe in community and connectedness too much for that. Even so, some days I feel disappointed that the church isn't what it could be or what it claims to be. Yet I know that the church is a very human institution, prone to all the same sins of other organizations. Even with the church's deficiencies, however, I don't feel compelled to leave it. It has been a shelter. It has been God's house. And I know that, no matter what, it is still inhabited by the Spirit. In fact, on many days I'm amazed at how successfully the Spirit uses this ragtag group of people who sometimes *do*, in fact, have their hearts in the right place.

But the spiritual life is a lot harder than I was led to believe or wistfully wanted when I saw it as the salvation from my conflicted upbringing. I know now that God lets us experience a holy longing even though it's uncomfortable. I also know that we often harm ourselves and others trying to avoid the tension this creates. I know that we won't understand it all until we see God face to face.

I do believe that God wants to give us the desires of our hearts as we commit ourselves to God's purposes. I don't think my own desires have been wrong—faith, family, self-development, community, children, love—what would be wrong with that? They are the dreams of all humans. Our longings are not idle bubbles that burst upon contact. Our longings are the deepest needs of our heart. They were planted there by God, and God has promised to fill them.

There are a few more things I'm positive about. I know it has been holy longing, the draw of God, which has led me along this path. I know I'm stronger in the broken places. I know God makes a way out of no way. I know Christ has made me whole. And I know I can't turn away, for I where else would I go? As the disciples said, "You have the words of eternal life."

I know that holy longing has kept me sane, functioning, productive, and always striving for more. I know that God has employed me and given meaning to my life, using all the disparate experiences, pains, and confusion for my own benefit and the benefit of others. I don't think God brought on those problems, but like a creative artist, God can make something beautiful out of the scraps and apparent trash of life. I know that God used the need and love of a little stranger—who is now one of the most important people in my life—to lead me on. I know it's not wrong to long for community. This is what the Kingdom or Realm of God is all about.

Perhaps the most important thing I have learned is this: It is only love that can move you beyond guilt, despair, and broken dreams. It doesn't matter where you direct your love—a child, a spouse, a community, some kind of service—as long as this love's light has been kindled at God's flame. Even if it starts as only a spark, it will grow. And that's how I've come to realize that, no matter how many dreams smash in front of you, if you follow the lure of love, God will use that love to make you whole.

Ellis Island

Well, actually, there's one more thing. Even though I'm only an adopted child of the Protestant culture, I am like all the other rationalistic mainstream types in one important way: I don't expect too many miracles, I don't have beatific visions, and I really can't claim many transcendent spiritual experiences. But I had one anyway one day, while visiting my friend Dori in New York City.

I decided to take a tour of Ellis Island. Although she wanted to go, since her ancestors came through this portal as well, at the last minute Dori had to work. The advantage of going alone was that I could spend as much time as I liked pondering the exhibits, since I'm one of those people who likes to read every word. I took the ferry over, trying to imagine what it would have been like to come across the ocean by ship, see the Statue of Liberty, and then disembark at Ellis. I entered the large main doors, trying to feel what my ethnic ancestors felt. The great hall immediately inside was intimidating. Back then, it would have been even more so—filled with anxious, tired people.

I walked slowly along the various stations, putting myself into the scene. I knew that, after a long and uncomfortable sea voyage, they would arrive with high hopes. But before they could really step foot in America, they would have to be evaluated. I tried to imagine how scared and possibly demeaned they must have felt. They would have their eyes, hearing, and intelligence tested. They would worry that one of the family might be sent back without the others. With a few family treasures and the minimal amount of money required to enter, they would have very few resources, family, or friends in the new place.

As I went around to the exhibits, trying to put myself in their place, I had a growing feeling of dismay. Here were my ancestors, people who had sacrificed so much to come here to improve their lives. But they also expected to find a more hospitable place to practice their religion, maintain their personal dignity, and escape prejudice. Given all they had done, I began to wonder what they would think of me. By now I had been at Ellis Island for several hours. Because I went so slowly, used my imagination, and had no one around me to impress or worry about, I was able to focus intently. Inside myself I entered a liminal space where time was suspended and my receptivity enhanced.

Fully in the moment, I glanced upward and saw large posters of various unnamed immigrants. There were clearly many Jews and Italians among the photographs. Their eyes were tired, intense, and focused. Suddenly, I felt they were watching me. So in my heart, I addressed them:

Here I am. I am from you. I know I've worked hard and
achieved some things. But I wonder what you would
actually think of me, if we could meet now? Would you
even recognize me as one of your own? Would you be
disappointed that I have deserted your religion and
your way of life? Would you be shocked that someone
like me has resulted from all your efforts? I'm sorry
for abandoning what you worked so hard to preserve.

As I silently said this, I thought I saw their faces soften,
and begin to glow. Now—don't get me wrong—I didn't actually hear voices. But in my heart, I thought I felt an answer
from them. This is what I felt they said to me:

Oh, no. We don't feel that way at all. It's hard to
believe that someone who came from us could get to
where you are. Imagine . . . to be a professor, to write
books, to teach. All right, being a Protestant minister
is a bit more than we expected . . . but . . . okay, we
can live with it. This is more than we had hoped to
achieve. How wonderful that this could have resulted
from our poor backgrounds and efforts. It was worth
all our sacrifices. America has not been a disappoint-
ment. We're amazed and we're proud of you!

It was a surprising message, and it felt like a benediction.
In fact, it startled me, for in my own limited perception, I
would find it hard to imagine that these ancestors could
actually accept me and even be proud. My lifelong confusion, shame, and guilt seemed to melt a little bit more. Their
message—coming unexpected and unbidden—contradicted
my basic instincts. I had to take it more seriously than simply
wishful thinking. Instead, there was something truthful and

profound about the experience. Standing there looking up at them, I suddenly realized it is all right that I feel Italian Catholic, Jewish, and Protestant all at the same time. I have not deserted my roots but have incorporated them into a new thing. It felt like another moment of grace.

Three Recent Snapshots
of Bloomfield Avenue

For a long time, I couldn't bear to go back to Bloomfield Avenue. Even when I visited New Jersey, I avoided Newark completely. I knew that our whole Italian world was gone, and it was too much for me. Finally, however, a professional commitment brought me back again. As a member of the Workgroup on Constructive Theology, I was asked to write an article on Newark for our project on urban theology. "No, not Newark, anywhere else, but not there," I protested, but they insisted I was the logical person to do it.

When we toured Newark for our research, I decided to show them where I had grown up. From the safety of the car, I pointed out the grubby streets of my childhood and especially our former shop on Bloomfield Avenue, now a laundromat. I was too embarrassed to ask what they thought, but I imagine they were surprised, since most of these lifelong Protestants had professional parents and suburban childhoods. But the article they inspired me to write not only forced me to give Newark another look but also started me writing this book.

On my next visit—with my son, David—I got a bit closer. This time we parked and got out to look. The street is still filled with small mom-and-pop businesses and just as urban-gritty as ever, but it is primarily Hispanic now. I felt comfortable on the street, but David kept looking over his shoulder, clearly nervous. "We don't fit in here, Mom," he said. After we'd stood outside the building for a few minutes and I pointed out my former bedroom window upstairs, he insisted on leaving.

On my third visit, I actually made it inside the building that once had housed our bakery. This time I brought my fiancé, Joseph (Jose Luis) Mas, a Cuban refugee—now an attorney who works in Columbus with immigrants. There was something oddly appropriate about his returning with me to my old world—once Italian immigrant, now Hispanic immigrant.

It was so strange when we first entered—all those washers and dryers where pastry display cases once had been. At first, I was overwhelmed with a sense of loss, but as I looked around, I noticed that the flooring, ceiling, and mirrored walls were just the same. Suddenly, the past and the present collided inside my head and I stood there transfixed, almost expecting my mother to call out to me from behind the counter.

The Latinas doing their laundry looked at me, clearly puzzled, and the manager came over to ask what we wanted. Joe used his Spanish to explain who I was, and the man graciously took us to the back of the shop. He showed us the former work and oven rooms which were now his apartment. The kitchen was completely transformed except for the same sink we had used—they hadn't been able to remove it, he said. I remembered all the cups and plates we had washed there when we had our rest breaks in that small room.

We didn't stay long. The man was very kind, but this was not my world anymore. I did not like being an outsider in what had once been my home. I did feel comforted, however, that my old environment was still giving newcomers a foothold in America. And I imagined that there were probably children in upstairs apartments at that very moment, wondering who they would become someday.

There is another consolation. Whenever I get nostalgic, I can watch reruns of *The Sopranos*. Filmed on location in New Jersey, this HBO series has made Newark and Bloomfield Avenue famous. In fact, the opening credits show a quick view of the church that was so spiritually formative for me, Sacred Heart Cathedral. Sometimes one's past and present come together in odd, unexpected ways.

Books by Linda Mercadante

Victims and Sinners: Spiritual Roots of Addiction and Recovery. Westminster John Knox Press, 1996.

Gender, Doctrine and God: The Shakers and Contemporary Theology. Abingdon Press, 1990.

From Hierarchy to Equality: A Comparison of Past and Present Interpretations of 1 Cor 11:2–16 in Relation to the Changing Status of Women in Society. GMH Books, Regent College, 1978.